THE FOLGER LIBRARY SHAKESPEARE

Designed to make Shakespeare's classic plays available to the general reader, each edition contains a reliable text with modernized spelling and punctuation, scene-by-scene plot summaries, and explanatory notes clarifying obscure and obsolete expressions. An interpretive essay and accounts of Shakespeare's life and theater form an instructive preface to each play.

Louis B. Wright, General Editor, was the Director of the Folger Shakespeare Library from 1948 until his retirement in 1968. He is the author of *Middle-Class Culture in Elizabethan England, Religion and Empire, Shakespeare for Everyman,* and many other books and essays on the history and literature of the Tudor and Stuart periods.

Virginia Lamar, Assistant Editor, served as research assistant to the Director and Executive Secretary of the Folger Shakespeare Library from 1946 until her death in 1968. She is the author of *English Dress in the Age of Shakespeare* and *Travel and Roads in England,* and coeditor of William Strachey's *Historie of Travell into Virginia Britania.*

The Folger Shakespeare Library

The Folger Library General Reader's Shakespeare

THE HISTORY OF

HENRY THE FOURTH

[PART 1]

by

WILLIAM SHAKESPEARE

WASHINGTON SQUARE PRESS
PUBLISHED BY POCKET BOOKS NEW YORK

WSP

A Washington Square Press Publication of
POCKET BOOKS, a Simon & Schuster division of
GULF & WESTERN CORPORATION
1230 Avenue of the Americas, New York, N.Y. 10020

ISBN: 0-671-41521-2

First Pocket Books printing January, 1961

25 24 23 22 21 20

WASHINGTON SQUARE PRESS, WSP and colophon are
trademarks of Simon & Schuster.

Printed in the U.S.A.

Preface

This edition of *Henry the Fourth, Part 1*, is designed to make available a readable text of one of Shakespeare's most popular plays. In the centuries since Shakespeare many changes have occurred in the meanings of words, and some clarification of Shakespeare's vocabulary may be helpful. To provide the reader with necessary notes in the most accessible format, we have placed them on the pages facing the text that they explain. We have tried to make these notes as brief and simple as possible. Preliminary to the text we have also included a brief statement of essential information about Shakespeare and his stage. Readers desiring more detailed information should refer to the books suggested in the references, and if still further information is needed, the bibliographies in those books will provide the necessary clues to the literature of the subject.

The early texts of all of Shakespeare's plays provide only inadequate stage directions, and it is conventional for modern editors to add many that clarify the action. Such additions, and additions to entrances, are placed in square brackets.

All illustrations are from material in the Folger Library collections.

L. B. W.
V. A. L.

May 28, 1960

The Beginning of a Dramatic Epic

In *Henry IV, Part 1,* Shakespeare gives us the first
play of a trilogy that has for its central theme the
deeds of one of England's most popular heroes,
Henry V. In the opening play, we see Henry as
Prince Hal, at first an unregenerate scapegrace, who
redeems a rowdy life by his heroism on the field at
Shrewsbury; but even early in the play the author
provides clues to the Prince's later evolution.
Whether Shakespeare had in mind a complete and
well-defined plan for three plays when he sat down
to compose the first part of *Henry IV* is a matter of
debate among scholars. But it is clear that he did
not intend to stop with the success of the King's
forces at Shrewsbury. The subject contained too
much of interest to Elizabethan audiences, and
Shakespeare was too thrifty a dramatist to abandon
so rich a vein at that point. Even had he not
planned other plays on the subject, the reception
of *Henry IV, Part 1,* was so encouraging that he
could hardly have refused to write a sequel. Before Shakespeare was through with the theme he
had produced a second part to *Henry IV, Henry V,*
and *The Merry Wives of Windsor,* all of which are
in some fashion related. The three plays on the life

and deeds of Henry V form a dramatic epic which stirred the blood of Shakespeare's contemporaries and continued to appeal to the patriotism of Englishmen for many generations.

For the date of composition and performance of *Henry IV, Part 1*, older scholars reached fairly general agreement upon 1597 or 1598 at the latest. In the New Arden edition of this play (1960), Professor Arthur R. Humphreys concludes that the play was composed sometime in 1596 and first acted in the winter of 1596–1597. He also thinks that the second part of *Henry IV* followed hard on the performance of the first and dates from late in 1597. Accepting the arguments of Mr. Leslie Hotson in *Shakespeare versus Shallow,* he agrees that there is good reason to believe that Shakespeare hurriedly devised a version of *The Merry Wives of Windsor* for a celebration at the installation of Knights of the Garter in May, 1597, when Lord Hunsdon, then Lord Chamberlain and the patron of Shakespeare's company, was made a Knight of the Garter. The text of *The Merry Wives* that has come down to us, however, shows revisions at a later date. The legend that Queen Elizabeth was so taken with the humor of Falstaff that she requested a play showing the fat knight in love may have some basis in fact. This chronology would put the composition and performance of *The Merry Wives* earlier than that of *Henry V,* which came in 1598–1599. It is entirely possible that the popularity of the Falstaffian comedy was such that Shakespeare was induced to interrupt the sequence of his epic to please the Queen and the court with Falstaff's misadventures as a Lothario.

Although the comedy elements in all three Henry plays vastly entertained Shakespeare's audiences, as they still entertain us, the history embodied in these plays was of paramount interest to Tudor audiences, who were not unaware of a parallel between Henry Bolingbroke and Henry Tudor, or between the victories of Henry V and the glory that had been England's in the defeat of the Spaniards in 1588. Englishmen of the late sixteenth century were concerned with their own history. A nation, like an individual, looks back with renewed interest upon its past when it attains prosperity and power. By the last decade of the sixteenth century, England had come to maturity and had taken its place as a first-class power among the nations of Europe. And its historians, its lyrical and epic poets, and its dramatists all ransacked the country's past for themes which could be used both to please and to instruct their fellow men.

Shakespeare had already paved the way for *Henry IV, Part 1*, with his production of *Richard II*, which had reached the stage two or three years before. In that play, written under the influence of Marlowe's *Edward II*, Shakespeare concentrates his interest upon the character of the poetic and dreamy Richard in contrast with that of practical and efficient Henry Bolingbroke. This play is a study in the qualities demanded of a king, and though Shake-

speare the poet treated Richard with a certain
amount of sympathy, Shakespeare the Elizabethan
appreciated the efficiency of Bolingbroke. The sixteenth century valued sovereigns who had the
strength and power to rule and to maintain order in
the commonwealth. The tradition of anarchy that
the Wars of the Roses bequeathed to later times was
never forgotten by Tudor Englishmen and they
dreaded weakness in the sovereign that might lead

Henry IV.
From John Taylor, *All the
Works* (1630).

to the return of political chaos. The Elizabethan Englishman was not a starry-eyed political idealist. Indeed, he had a certain amount of sympathy with the doctrines of Machiavelli and understood the practical necessities of "policy" in the management of affairs of state. When Shakespeare portrays Henry Bolingbroke as the cold-blooded and efficient agent in Richard's ruin, he does not see him as a villain. Richard had failed the commonwealth and had brought down upon himself the forces that toppled his throne.

But even if Richard had shown himself an incompetent ruler, Henry Bolingbroke, who deposed and killed him, in seizing the crown for himself had committed a great sin by laying profane hands on the Lord's anointed. "There's such divinity doth hedge a king/That treason can but peep to what it would," Shakespeare later made King Claudius say in *Hamlet*. Even where provocation was overwhelming, so great was the mystical divinity surrounding royalty that violence against the sovereign was a sin demanding the utmost expiation. A genuine repugnance to doing violence to an anointed sovereign helps explain Queen Elizabeth's long hesitation in bringing Mary of Scotland to judgment, even after she was convinced of Mary's plots against her own life.

When *Henry IV* opens, the King reveals his plan for a crusade against the Saracens, long in contemplation but now blocked once more by the threat of civil strife. Later we learn that the crusade

was designed to serve as expiation for King Henry's
sin against Richard, the anointed ruler. Indeed, the
disasters that hover over Henry's realm are, he be-
lieves, a punishment sent by God upon him because of this unpurged guilt. Even the Prince's irre-
sponsible conduct he interprets as one of the afflic-
tions caused by his sin, as he makes clear in the
reprimand delivered to the Prince in the second
scene of Act III.

This scene marks the turning point in the characterization of Prince Hal, hitherto portrayed as a
madcap roisterer. Although he does not immediately abandon Falstaff and his old cronies, we have
his promise to his father that he will play the role
of a true prince of the blood.

> I will redeem all this on Percy's head
> And, in the closing of some glorious day,
> Be bold to tell you that I am your son,
> When I will wear a garment all of blood,
> And stain my favors in a bloody mask,
> Which, washed away, shall scour my shame
>   with it.
> .   .   .   .
> This in the name of God I promise here;
> The which if He be pleased I shall perform,
> I do beseech your Majesty may salve
> The long-grown wounds of my intemperance.
> If not, the end of life cancels all bands,
> And I will die a hundred thousand deaths
> Ere break the smallest parcel of this vow.

If these words taken out of context smack of grandiloquent heroics to a modern ear, to an Elizabethan they had an authentic ring. From this point onward, Shakespeare's audience could expect Prince Hal to play the part assigned to an epic hero. Implicit in the three Henry plays are lessons in kingship which Elizabethan audiences could understand and appreciate as a modern reader understands political doctrine revealed in the daily newspaper. The serious portions of the play provided Elizabethans with matter that was not only entertaining but also full of desirable instruction.

Shakespeare inherited a dramatic tradition that was full of clownery and horseplay. In the drama that preceded him, even in serious religious drama, comic elements were frequently interspersed with serious scenes. In the Scriptural play of the Flood, for example, Noah might beat his sharp-tongued wife black and blue for the comic delectation of the audience, and in the later morality plays, the Vice was an amusing clown who provided comic relief. Chronicle plays, and even tragedies, that preceded Shakespeare's work, sometimes had comic subplots or irrelevant comic characters completely unrelated to the main action. One of Shakespeare's achievements in dramatic construction was the welding of his comic subplot to the rest of the play. In *Henry IV,* the comic scenes with Falstaff are not disjointed bits of clownery inserted for the groundlings, but they are woven into the play to form an integral part of the structure. The unifying element is the Prince, and his reaction to the comic plot serves to further the development and revelation of his character.

The comedy in *Henry IV* has amused the world from Shakespeare's day until our own. It conveys a type of humor that is timeless and immortal, and Falstaff's japes and jests will be as fresh tomorrow as they were in the England of Elizabeth I. The comedy is a comedy of humor as distinguished from the comedy of mere wit, a comedy of incongruity

Henry V.
From John Taylor, *All the Works* (1630).

and of situation instead of being dependent upon wordplay alone. It is earthy, substantial, and of universal understanding as opposed to the brittle wit revealed in the wisecrack of a television comic. While the witty wisecrack excites a flicker of gaiety when it is first heard, it will not bear repetition, whereas the doings of Falstaff and his crew induce deep-seated laughter that increases rather than diminishes with the telling. No matter how many times one has heard Falstaff's soliloquy on honor, it is always funny, and his observation of "Lord, Lord, how this world is given to lying" has become part of our comic proverbial lore. In the presence of Falstaff's humor, pomposities and pretensions shrivel to their proper dimensions.

Victorian critics who found Falstaff too amusing to dismiss were sometimes uneasy in their consciences because of their love for a reprobate and a coward. As a result, they wasted much paper and ink attempting to whitewash Falstaff and to prove that he was not really a coward, all of which is of course beside the point. Shakespeare created a comic character, gave him as companions a group of tavern-haunters and rascals, and let the situations work themselves out in the amoral world of the comic theatre. We do not love Falstaff because we recognize him as someone we have known, for few of us have ever known a character like Falstaff, but he amuses us because he embodies characteristics that we recognize as common and, in certain situations, amusing traits and frailties of humankind.

A person without a sense of humor himself will perhaps find Falstaff merely a fat and untidy old man not above running away from danger. Upon a humorless person, a philosophic explanation of Falstaff will be wasted. Fortunately, most of mankind can laugh at the incongruities that Shakespeare provides in the portrayal of the Falstaff scenes, and few will demand a refutation of Falstaff's cowardice or a certificate of moral purity before they can accept him as a figure of fun. Falstaff and his ribald companions are characters of comedy and they have a long ancestry in the theatre. If Shakespeare breathes such life into them that some commentators feel a need to justify their actions in terms of everyday existence, that is merely a tribute to his skill in giving a sense of reality to his characters and scenes.

Although Falstaff and his crew are theatrical types who can be labeled and pigeonholed by students of the theatre, they move about in an English setting and provide an atmosphere of tavern life that has been as pervasive as Shakespeare's legacy of historical interpretation. When someone alludes to Shakespeare and Ben Jonson engaging in a drinking bout at the Mermaid Tavern, the chances are that the imaginary scene flashed upon one's mind is conditioned by the Boar's Head in *Henry IV*. Thanks to Shakespeare's settings in these comic scenes, we have an imaginary concept of English low life over which Falstaff inevitably presides. Falstaff and the Boar's Head are realities in our literary inheritance.

The comic scenes, desirable as they are in themselves as amusement for the spectators, serve a much deeper purpose in the drama. In the education of Prince Hal, they act as a humanizing influence. Falstaff himself makes the point in *Henry IV, Part 2*, that the drinking of a good store of sack has "in Hal warmed the cold Bolingbrokian blood." Professor Humphreys, in the introduction to the New Arden edition, makes this cogent observation: "Serious and comic themes are entwined by other echoes and links. They unite in a vision of national life both broad and deep, and are expressed in a style of extraordinary energy, whether in serious verse or comic prose. This vision of national life has its comprehensive geographical range and its long perspectives of time; it looks into the future and it reaches into the past, for retrospection is as integral to reminiscences of a comic past as to those of tragic history. The great idea of England is woven from all these themes." In our imaginative re-creation of the English tradition, the scenes in the Boar's Head in Eastcheap are as important as the heroic words and deeds of King Henry V before Agincourt.

SOURCES AND DRAMATIC TREATMENT

For the main outlines of his historical plot, Shakespeare turned to the easiest of sources, the second edition of Raphael Holinshed's *Chronicles of Eng-*

land, Scotland, and Ireland (1587), but that was not his only source. An old play, *The Famous Victories of Henry the Fifth,* published in 1598, had been performed much earlier by the Queen's Men and was known to Shakespeare. It is a crude episodic drama full of horseplay and foolery, but from it Shakespeare may have got his own ideas for the alternation of comic and serious scenes. *The Famous Victories* has among its characters Sir John Oldcastle, the prototype of Falstaff, and other minor figures who do not come from Holinshed. One has only to read *The Famous Victories* to gain a fresh appreciation of Shakespeare's skill in transforming second-rate material into a work of art. Shakespeare also made some use of Samuel Daniel's *Civil Wars* (1595), a long narrative poem, which parallels a few situations in Shakespeare's play that are not in Holinshed, for example, in bringing Prince Hal and Hotspur into combat and making Hotspur a young man, nearer the Prince's age. Historically, the Prince was only sixteen years old at the time of the Battle of Shrewsbury, and Hotspur was twenty-three years older, older even than King Henry IV. Shakespeare's emphasis on Hotspur as a dashing youth, at which Daniel had hinted, made a dramatic contrast with Prince Hal in the play. Information about Prince Hal's riotous youth Shakespeare may have found in John Stow's *Annals of England* (1592) and his other chronicles, which make the Prince's escapades more specific than Holinshed.

As usual in his history plays, Shakespeare took such liberties with facts as the requirements of the stage dictated. Not only did he make Prince Hal and Hotspur about the same age, but he invented the epic combat between them and made the Prince slay Hotspur. The fact is that no one knows how Hotspur died. The Prince's rescue of his father is also an invention. Shakespeare is sometimes careless about facts, or perpetuates error in his sources. For example, he follows Holinshed in confusing Edmund Mortimer, the fifth Earl of March, with his uncle, Sir Edmund Mortimer, who had been kept a prisoner by Owen Glendower. In general, however, the play gives the generally accepted facts concerning the historical events that transpired during the time of action, an indefinite period in 1402 until July, 1403.

Falstaff's ancestry is historical, and that fact caused Shakespeare some difficulty. In the first acted version of *Henry IV, Part 1*, Falstaff was called Sir John Oldcastle, a name used in *The Famous Victories*, whence Shakespeare probably derived it. But the historical Sir John Oldcastle was not only a hero and a Lollard martyr, who was executed for his religion during the reign of Henry V, but he was an ancestor of William Brooke, Lord Cobham. Either William Brooke or his son, Henry Brooke, who inherited the title, complained about Shakespeare's travesty of their ancestor, and he had to change it. In choosing the name Falstaff, Shakespeare again used a name that was historical, perhaps because he wanted to keep his play from departing too far from historical verisimilitude. Falstaff is an adaptation of Sir John Fastolfe, an actual soldier against the French, who had been already represented unfairly as a coward in the first part of *Henry VI.* If any descendants of Sir John Fastolfe protested, their complaints had no effect.

POPULARITY ON THE STAGE

From the time of its first production, *Henry IV, Part 1,* has remained almost continuously a favorite with playgoers. The fact that eight quarto versions were printed before the closing of the theatres in 1640 is in itself an indication of the popularity of the play. A manuscript now in the Folger Library shows that sometime in the first half of the seventeenth century an adapter telescoped both parts of *Henry IV* into a single play, perhaps for a private performance. The manuscript has corrections in the hand of a country gentleman of Kent, Sir Edward Dering, who died in 1644. On the stage, the play was constantly revived both in the public playhouses and at court. After the Restoration, *Henry IV, Part 1,* was one of the first of Shakespeare's plays performed and it continued to hold the stage. Thomas Betterton, who made an adaptation of the play, took the part of Hotspur, until he grew too old and fat, whereupon he shifted to Falstaff.

In the eighteenth century, *Henry IV, Part 1,* was one of the most popular of Shakespeare's plays.

Garrick produced the play at Drury Lane with considerable success, though he himself did not prove a convincing Hotspur. The most famous of the eighteenth-century Falstaffs was James Quin, who made a great reputation in the part. Indeed, the role of Falstaff has been a favorite with most actors who have had any skill in comedy. In the nineteenth and twentieth centuries, *Henry IV, Part 1*, continued to hold its audiences. In 1939 Margaret Webster produced in New York a highly successful version of *Henry IV, Part 1*, with Maurice Evans as Falstaff. A production of *Henry IV, Part 1*, at the Phoenix Theatre in New York, which opened early in 1960, proved so popular, without the drawing power of any "star" names in the cast, that the company decided to produce Part 2 as well and play both parts alternately.

This play has been a favorite with actors because of the variety of characterization that it offers and the opportunities for more than one star to shine. Prince Hal, Hotspur, Falstaff, the King himself, and many of the smaller parts, are all roles that give actors an opportunity to exhibit their talents.

THE TEXT

Although six quartos (and one variant fragment in the Folger Library) preceded the publication of the Folio text of *Henry IV, Part 1*, in 1623, the later quartos seem to have been printed successively from one another, despite the fact that they sometimes claim on title pages to be "newly corrected." The First Folio text seems to derive from Quarto 5. The most authoritative text is therefore the First Quarto, which is the basis of the present text.

THE AUTHOR

As early as 1598 Shakespeare was so well known as a literary and dramatic craftsman that Francis Meres, in his *Palladis Tamia: Wits Treasury*, referred in flattering terms to him as "mellifluous and honey-tongued Shakespeare," famous for his *Venus and Adonis*, his *Lucrece*, and "his sugared sonnets," which were circulating "among his private friends." Meres observes further that "as Plautus and Seneca are accounted the best for comedy and tragedy among the Latins, so Shakespeare among the English is the most excellent in both kinds for the stage," and he mentions a dozen plays that had made a name for Shakespeare. He concludes with the remark "that the Muses would speak with Shakespeare's fine filed phrase if they would speak English."

To those acquainted with the history of the Elizabethan and Jacobean periods, it is incredible that anyone should be so naïve or ignorant as to doubt the reality of Shakespeare as the author of the plays that bear his name. Yet so much nonsense has been written about other "candidates" for the plays that it is well to remind readers that no credible evidence that would stand up in a court of law has ever been adduced to prove either that Shakespeare did not write his plays or that anyone else wrote them. All the theories offered for the authorship of Francis Bacon, the Earl of Derby, the Earl of Oxford, the Earl of Hertford, Christopher Marlowe, and a score of other candidates are mere conjectures spun from the active imaginations of persons who confuse hypothesis and conjecture with evidence.

As Meres' statement of 1598 indicates, Shakespeare was already a popular playwright whose name carried weight at the box office. The obvious reputation of Shakespeare as early as 1598 makes the effort to prove him a myth one of the most absurd in the history of human perversity.

The anti-Shakespeareans talk darkly about a plot of vested interests to maintain the authorship of Shakespeare. Nobody has any vested interest in Shakespeare, but every scholar is interested in the truth and in the quality of evidence advanced by special pleaders who set forth hypotheses in place of facts.

The anti-Shakespeareans base their arguments upon a few simple premises, all of them false. These false premises are that Shakespeare was an unlettered yokel without any schooling, that nothing is known about Shakespeare, and that only a noble lord or the equivalent in background could have written the plays. The facts are that more is known about Shakespeare than about most dramatists of

his day, that he had a very good education, acquired in the Stratford Grammar School, that the
plays show no evidence of profound book learning, and that the knowledge of kings and courts
evident in the plays is no greater than any intelli-
gent young man could have picked up at second
hand. Most anti-Shakespeareans are naïve and be-
tray an obvious snobbery. The author of their
favorite plays, they imply, must have had a college
diploma framed and hung on his study wall like
the one in their dentist's office, and obviously so
great a writer must have had a title or some equally
significant evidence of exalted social background.
They forget that genius has a way of cropping up
in unexpected places and that none of the great
creative writers of the world got his inspiration in
a college or university course.

William Shakespeare was the son of John Shakespeare of Stratford-upon-Avon, a substantial citizen
of that small but busy market town in the center
of the rich agricultural county of Warwick. John
Shakespeare kept a shop, what we would call a
general store; he dealt in wool and other produce
and gradually acquired property. As a youth, John
Shakespeare had learned the trade of glover and
leather worker. There is no contemporary evidence
that the elder Shakespeare was a butcher, though
the anti-Shakespeareans like to talk about the ignorant "butcher's boy of Stratford." Their only
evidence is a statement by gossipy John Aubrey,
more than a century after William Shakespeare's

birth, that young William followed his father's trade, and when he killed a calf, "he would do it in a high style and make a speech." We would like to believe the story true, but Aubrey is not a very credible witness.

John Shakespeare probably continued to operate a farm at Snitterfield that his father had leased. He married Mary Arden, daughter of his father's landlord, a man of some property. The third of their eight children was William, baptized on April 26, 1564, and probably born three days before. At least, it is conventional to celebrate April 23 as his birthday.

The Stratford records give considerable information about John Shakespeare. We know that he held several municipal offices including those of alderman and mayor. In 1580 he was in some sort of legal difficulty and was fined for neglecting a summons of the Court of Queen's Bench requiring him to appear at Westminster and be bound over to keep the peace.

As a citizen and alderman of Stratford, John Shakespeare was entitled to send his son to the grammar school free. Though the records are lost, there can be no reason to doubt that this is where young William received his education. As any student of the period knows, the grammar schools provided the basic education in Latin learning and literature. The Elizabethan grammar school is not to be confused with modern grammar schools. Many cultivated men of the day received all their formal education in the grammar schools. At the universities in this period a student would have received little training that would have inspired him to be a creative writer. At Stratford young Shakespeare would have acquired a familiarity with Latin and some little knowledge of Greek. He would have read Latin authors and become acquainted with the plays of Plautus and Terence. Undoubtedly, in this period of his life he received that stimulation to read and explore for himself the world of ancient and modern history which he later utilized in his plays. The youngster who does not acquire this type of intellectual curiosity *before* college days rarely develops as a result of a college course the kind of mind Shakespeare demonstrated. His learning in books was anything but profound, but he clearly had the probing curiosity that sent him in search of information, and he had a keenness in the observation of nature and of humankind that finds reflection in his poetry.

There is little documentation for Shakespeare's boyhood. There is little reason why there should be. Nobody knew that he was going to be a dramatist about whom any scrap of information would be prized in the centuries to come. He was merely an active and vigorous youth of Stratford, perhaps assisting his father in his business, and no Boswell bothered to write down facts about him. The most important record that we have is a marriage license issued by the Bishop of Worcester on November 28, 1582, to permit William Shakespeare to marry

Anne Hathaway, seven or eight years his senior; furthermore, the Bishop permitted the marriage after reading the banns only once instead of three times, evidence of the desire for haste. The need was explained on May 26, 1583, when the christening of Susanna, daughter of William and Anne Shakespeare, was recorded at Stratford. Two years later, on February 2, 1585, the records show the birth of twins to the Shakespeares, a boy and a girl who were christened Hamnet and Judith.

What William Shakespeare was doing in Stratford during the early years of his married life, or when he went to London, we do not know. It has been conjectured that he tried his hand at schoolteaching, but that is a mere guess. There is a legend that he left Stratford to escape a charge of poaching in the park of Sir Thomas Lucy of Charlecote, but there is no proof of this. There is also a legend that when first he came to London, he earned his living by holding horses outside a playhouse and presently was given employment inside, but there is nothing better than eighteenth-century hearsay for this. How Shakespeare broke into the London theatres as a dramatist and actor we do not know. But lack of information is not surprising, for Elizabethans did not write their autobiographies, and we know even less about the lives of many writers and some men of affairs than we know about Shakespeare. By 1592 he was so well established and popular that he incurred the envy of the dramatist and pamphleteer Robert Greene, who referred to him as an "upstart crow . . . in his own conceit the only Shake-scene in a country." From this time onward, contemporary allusions and references in legal documents enable the scholar to chart Shakespeare's career with greater accuracy than is possible with most other Elizabethan dramatists.

By 1594 Shakespeare was a member of the company of actors known as the Lord Chamberlain's Men. After the accession of James I, in 1603, the company would have the sovereign for their patron and would be known as the King's Men. During the period of its greatest prosperity, this company would have as its principal theatres the Globe and the Blackfriars. Shakespeare was both an actor and a shareholder in the company. Tradition has assigned him such acting roles as Adam in *As You Like It* and the Ghost in *Hamlet*, a modest place on the stage that suggests that he may have had other duties in the management of the company. Such conclusions, however, are based on surmise.

What we do know is that his plays were popular and that he was highly successful in his vocation. His first play may have been *The Comedy of Errors*, acted perhaps in 1591. Certainly this was one of his earliest plays. The three parts of *Henry VI* were acted sometime between 1590 and 1592. Critics are not in agreement about precisely how much Shakespeare wrote of these three plays. *Richard III* probably dates from 1593. From this time onward, Shakespeare's plays followed on the stage in rapid succession: *Titus Andronicus, The Taming* of the Shrew, The Two Gentlemen of Verona, Love's Labour's Lost, Romeo and Juliet, Richard II, A Midsummer Night's Dream, King John, The Merchant of Venice, Henry IV (Parts 1 and 2), Much Ado About Nothing, Henry V, Julius Cæsar, As You Like It, Twelfth Night, Hamlet, The Merry Wives of Windsor, All's Well That Ends Well, Measure for Measure, Othello, King Lear, and nine others that followed before Shakespeare retired completely, about 1613.

In the course of his career in London, he made enough money to enable him to retire to Stratford with a competence. His purchase on May 4, 1597, of New Place, then the second-largest dwelling in Stratford, a "pretty house of brick and timber," with a handsome garden, indicates his increasing prosperity. There his wife and children lived while he busied himself in the London theatres. The summer before he acquired New Place, his life was darkened by the death of his only son, Hamnet, a child of eleven. In May, 1602, Shakespeare purchased one hundred and seven acres of fertile farmland near Stratford and a few months later bought a cottage and garden across the alley from New Place. About 1611, he seems to have returned permanently to Stratford, for the next year a legal document refers to him as "William Shakespeare of Stratford-upon-Avon . . . gentleman." To achieve the desired appellation of gentleman, William Shakespeare had seen to it that the College of Heralds in 1596 granted his father a coat of arms. In one step he thus became a second-generation gentleman.

Shakespeare's daughter Susanna made a good match in 1607 with Dr. John Hall, a prominent and prosperous Stratford physician. His second daughter, Judith, did not marry until she was thirty-two years old, and then, under somewhat scandalous circumstances, she married Thomas Quiney, a Stratford vintner. On March 25, 1616, Shakespeare made his will, bequeathing his landed property to Susanna, £300 to Judith, certain sums to other relatives, and his second-best bed to his wife, Anne. Much has been made of the second-best bed, but the legacy probably indicates only that Anne liked that particular bed. Shakespeare, following the practice of the time, may have already arranged with Susanna for his wife's care. Finally, on April 23, 1616, the anniversary of his birth, William Shakespeare died, and he was buried on April 25 within the chancel of Trinity Church, as befitted an honored citizen. On August 6, 1623, a few months before the publication of the collected edition of Shakespeare's plays, Anne Shakespeare joined her husband in death.

THE PUBLICATION OF HIS PLAYS

During his lifetime Shakespeare made no effort to publish any of his plays, though eighteen appeared in print in single-play editions known as quartos. Some of these are corrupt versions known as "bad quartos." No quarto, so far as is known, had the author's approval. Plays were not considered "literature" any more than most radio and television scripts today are considered literature. Dramatists sold their plays outright to the theatrical companies and it was usually considered in the company's interest to keep plays from getting into print. To achieve a reputation as a man of letters, Shakespeare wrote his *Sonnets* and his narrative poems, *Venus and Adonis* and *The Rape of Lucrece*, but he probably never dreamed that his plays would establish his reputation as a literary genius. Only Ben Jonson, a man known for his colossal conceit, had the crust to call his plays *Works*, as he did when he published an edition in 1616. But men laughed at Ben Jonson.

After Shakespeare's death, two of his old colleagues in the King's Men, John Heminges and Henry Condell, decided that it would be a good thing to print, in more accurate versions than were then available, the plays already published and eighteen additional plays not previously published in quarto. In 1623 appeared *Mr. William Shakespeares Comedies, Histories, & Tragedies. Published according to the True Originall Copies. London. Printed by Isaac Iaggard and Ed. Blount.* This was the famous First Folio, a work that had the authority of Shakespeare's associates. The only play commonly attributed to Shakespeare that was omitted in the First Folio was *Pericles.* In their preface, "To the great Variety of Readers," Heminges and Condell state that whereas "you were abused with diverse stolen and surreptitious copies, maimed and deformed by the frauds and stealths of injurious impostors that exposed them, even those are now offered to your view cured and perfect of their limbs; and all the rest, absolute in their numbers, as he conceived them." What they used for printer's copy is one of the vexed problems of scholarship, and skilled bibliographers have devoted years of study to the question of the relation of the "copy" for the First Folio to Shakespeare's manuscripts. In some cases it is clear that the editors corrected printed quarto versions of the plays, probably by comparison with playhouse scripts. Whether these scripts were in Shakespeare's autograph is anybody's guess. No manuscript of any play in Shakespeare's handwriting has survived. Indeed, very few play manuscripts from this period by any author are extant. The Tudor and Stuart periods had not yet learned to prize autographs and authors' original manuscripts.

Since the First Folio contains eighteen plays not previously printed, it is the only source for these. For the other eighteen, which had appeared in quarto versions, the First Folio also has the authority of an edition prepared and overseen by Shakespeare's colleagues and professional associates. But since editorial standards in 1623 were far from strict, and Heminges and Condell were actors rather than editors by profession, the texts are sometimes careless. The printing and proofreading of the

First Folio also left much to be desired, and some garbled passages have to be corrected and emended. The "good quarto" texts have to be taken into account in preparing a modern edition.

Because of the great popularity of Shakespeare through the centuries, the First Folio has become a prized book, but it is not a very rare one, for it is estimated that 238 copies are extant. The Folger Shakespeare Library in Washington, D.C., has seventy-nine copies of the First Folio, collected by the founder, Henry Clay Folger, who believed that a collation of as many texts as possible would reveal significant facts about the text of Shakespeare's plays. Dr. Charlton Hinman, using an ingenious machine of his own invention for mechanical collating, has made many discoveries that throw light on Shakespeare's text and on printing practices of the day.

The probability is that the First Folio of 1623 had an edition of between 1,000 and 1,250 copies. It is believed that it sold for £1, which made it an expensive book, for £1 in 1623 was equivalent to something between $40 and $50 in modern purchasing power.

During the seventeenth century, Shakespeare was sufficiently popular to warrant three later editions in folio size, the Second Folio of 1632, the Third Folio of 1663–1664, and the Fourth Folio of 1685. The Third Folio added six other plays ascribed to Shakespeare, but these are apocryphal.

THE SHAKESPEAREAN THEATRE

The theatres in which Shakespeare's plays were performed were vastly different from those we know today. The stage was a platform that jutted out into the area now occupied by the first rows of seats on the main floor, what is called the "orchestra" in America and the "pit" in England. This platform had no curtain to come down at the ends of acts and scenes. And although simple stage properties were available, the Elizabethan theatre lacked both the machinery and the elaborate movable scenery of the modern theatre. In the rear of the platform stage was a curtained area that could be used as an inner room, a tomb, or any such scene that might be required. A balcony above this inner room, and perhaps balconies on the sides of the stage, could represent the upper deck of a ship, the entry to Juliet's room, or a prison window. A trap door in the stage provided an entrance for ghosts and devils from the nether regions, and a similar trap in the canopied structure over the stage, known as the "heavens," made it possible to let down angels on a rope. These primitive stage arrangements help to account for many elements in Elizabethan plays. For example, since there was no curtain, the dramatist frequently felt the necessity of writing into his play action to clear the stage at the ends of acts and scenes. The funeral march at the end of *Hamlet* is not there merely for atmosphere; Shakespeare had to get the corpses off the stage. The lack of scenery also freed the dramatist from undue concern about the exact location of his sets, and the physical relation of his various settings to each other did not have to be worked out with the same precision as in the modern theatre.

Before London had buildings designed exclusively for theatrical entertainment, plays were given in inns and taverns. The characteristic inn of the period had an inner courtyard with rooms opening onto balconies overlooking the yard. Players could set up their temporary stages at one end of the yard and audiences could find seats on the balconies out of the weather. The poorer sort could stand or sit on the cobblestones in the yard, which was open to the sky. The first theatres followed this construction, and throughout the Elizabethan period the large public theatres had a yard in front of the stage open to the weather, with two or three tiers of covered balconies extending around the theatre. This physical structure again influenced the writing of plays. Because a dramatist wanted the actors to be heard, he frequently wrote into his play orations that could be delivered with declamatory effect. He also provided spectacle, buffoonery, and broad jests to keep the riotous groundlings in the yard entertained and quiet.

In another respect the Elizabethan theatre differed greatly from ours. It had no actresses. All women's roles were taken by boys, sometimes recruited from the boys' choirs of the London

churches. Some of these youths acted their roles
with great skill and the Elizabethans did not seem
to be aware of any incongruity. The first actresses
on the professional English stage appeared after
the Restoration of Charles II, in 1660, when exiled
Englishmen brought back from France practices of
the French stage.

London in the Elizabethan period, as now, was
the center of theatrical interest, though wandering
actors from time to time traveled through the country performing in inns, halls, and the houses of the
nobility. The first professional playhouse, called
simply The Theatre, was erected by James Burbage,
father of Shakespeare's colleague Richard Burbage,
in 1576 on lands of the old Holywell Priory adjacent
to Finsbury Fields, a playground and park area
just north of the city walls. It had the advantage of
being outside the city's jurisdiction and yet was
near enough to be easily accessible. Soon after The
Theatre was opened, another playhouse called The
Curtain was erected in the same neighborhood.
Both of these playhouses had open courtyards and
were probably polygonal in shape.

About the time The Curtain opened, Richard
Farrant, Master of the Children of the Chapel
Royal at Windsor and of St. Paul's, conceived the
idea of opening a "private" theatre in the old monastery buildings of the Blackfriars, not far from
St. Paul's Cathedral in the heart of the city. This
theatre was ostensibly to train the choirboys in
plays for presentation at Court, but Farrant man-

aged to present plays to paying audiences and achieved considerable success until aristocratic neighbors complained and had the theatre closed. This first Blackfriars Theatre was significant, however, because it popularized the boy actors in a professional way and it paved the way for a second theatre in the Blackfriars, which Shakespeare's company took over more than thirty years later. By the last years of the sixteenth century, London had at least six professional theatres and still others were erected during the reign of James I.

The Globe Theatre, the playhouse that most people connect with Shakespeare, was erected early in 1599 on the Bankside, the area across the Thames from the city. Its construction had a dramatic beginning, for on the night of December 28, 1598, James Burbage's sons, Cuthbert and Richard, gathered together a crew who tore down the old theatre in Holywell and carted the timbers across the river to a site that they had chosen for a new playhouse. The reason for this clandestine operation was a row with the landowner over the lease to the Holywell property. The site chosen for the Globe was another playground outside of the city's jurisdiction, a region of somewhat unsavory character. Not far away was the Bear Garden, an amphitheatre devoted to the baiting of bears and bulls. This was also the region occupied by many houses of ill fame licensed by the Bishop of Winchester and the source of substantial revenue to him. But it was easily accessible either from London Bridge or by means

of the cheap boats operated by the London water-
men, and it had the great advantage of being beyond the authority of the Puritanical aldermen of
London, who frowned on plays because they lured
apprentices from work, filled their heads with improper ideas, and generally exerted a bad influence.
The aldermen also complained that the crowds
drawn together in the theatre helped to spread the
plague.

The Globe was the handsomest theatre up to its
time. It was a large building, apparently octagonal
in shape and open like its predecessors to the sky in
the center, but capable of seating a large audience
in its covered balconies. To erect and operate the
Globe, the Burbages organized a syndicate composed of the leading members of the dramatic
company, of which Shakespeare was a member.
Since it was open to the weather and depended on
natural light, plays had to be given in the afternoon. This caused no hardship in the long after-
noons of an English summer, but in the winter the
weather was a great handicap and discouraged all
except the hardiest. For that reason, in 1608 Shakespeare's company was glad to take over the lease
of the second Blackfriars Theatre, a substantial,
roomy hall reconstructed within the framework of
the old monastery building. This theatre was pro-
tected from the weather and its stage was artifi-
cially lighted by chandeliers of candles. This became the winter playhouse for Shakespeare's com-

pany and at once proved so popular that the congestion of traffic created an embarrassing problem. Stringent regulations had to be made for the movement of coaches in the vicinity. Shakespeare's company continued to use the Globe during the summer months. In 1613 a squib fired from a cannon during a performance of *Henry VIII* fell on the thatched roof and the Globe burned to the ground. The next year it was rebuilt.

London had other famous theatres. The Rose, just west of the Globe, was built by Philip Henslowe, a semiliterate denizen of the Bankside, who became one of the most important theatrical owners and producers of the Tudor and Stuart periods. What is more important for historians, he kept a detailed account book, which provides much of our information about theatrical history in his time. Another famous theatre on the Bankside was the Swan, which a Dutch priest, Johannes de Witt, visited in 1596. The crude drawing of the stage which he made was copied by his friend Arend van Buchell; it is one of the important pieces of contemporary evidence for theatrical construction. Among the other theatres, the Fortune, north of the city, on Golding Lane, and the Red Bull, even farther away from the city, off St. John's Street, were the most popular. The Red Bull, much frequented by apprentices, favored sensational and sometimes rowdy plays.

The actors who kept all of these theatres going were organized into companies under the protection of some noble patron. Traditionally actors had enjoyed a low reputation. In some of the ordinances they were classed as vagrants; in the phraseology of the time, "rogues, vagabonds, sturdy beggars, and common players" were all listed together as undesirables. To escape penalties often meted out to these characters, organized groups of actors managed to gain the protection of various personages of high degree. In the later years of Elizabeth's reign, a group flourished under the name of the Queen's Men; another group had the protection of the Lord Admiral and were known as the Lord Admiral's Men. Edward Alleyn, son-in-law of Philip Henslowe, was the leading spirit in the Lord Admiral's Men. Besides the adult companies, troupes of boy actors from time to time also enjoyed considerable popularity. Among these were the Children of Paul's and the Children of the Chapel Royal.

The company with which Shakespeare had a long association had for its first patron Henry Carey, Lord Hunsdon, the Lord Chamberlain, and hence they were known as the Lord Chamberlain's Men. After the accession of James I, they became the King's Men. This company was the great rival of the Lord Admiral's Men, managed by Henslowe and Alleyn.

All was not easy for the players in Shakespeare's time, for the aldermen of London were always eager for an excuse to close up the Blackfriars and any other theatres in their jurisdiction. The theatres outside the jurisdiction of London were not immune from interference, for they might be shut up by order of the Privy Council for meddling in politics or for various other offenses, or they might be closed in time of plague lest they spread infection. During plague times, the actors usually went on tour and played the provinces wherever they could find an audience. Particularly frightening were the plagues of 1592–1594 and 1613 when the theatres closed and the players, like many other Londoners, had to take to the country.

Though players had a low social status, they enjoyed great popularity, and one of the favorite forms of entertainment at Court was the performance of plays. To be commanded to perform at Court conferred great prestige upon a company of players, and printers frequently noted that fact when they published plays. Several of Shakespeare's plays were performed before the sovereign, and Shakespeare himself undoubtedly acted in some of these plays.

REFERENCES FOR FURTHER READING

Many readers will want suggestions for further reading about Shakespeare and his times. The literature in this field is enormous but a few references will serve as guides to further study. A simple and useful little book is Gerald Sanders, *A Shakespeare Primer* (New York, 1950). *A Companion to Shakespeare Studies*, edited by Harley Granville-Barker and G. B. Harrison (Cambridge, Eng., 1934) is a valuable guide. More detailed but still not too voluminous to be confusing is Hazelton Spencer, *The Art and Life of William Shakespeare* (New York, 1940) which, like Sanders' handbook, contains a brief annotated list of useful books on various aspects of the subject. The most detailed and scholarly work providing complete factual information about Shakespeare is Sir Edmund Chambers, *William Shakespeare: A Study of Facts and Problems* (2 vols., Oxford, 1930). For detailed, factual information about the Elizabethan and seventeenth-century stages, the definitive reference works are Sir Edmund Chambers, *The Elizabethan Stage* (4 vols., Oxford, 1923) and Gerald E. Bentley, *The Jacobean and Caroline Stage* (5 vols., Oxford, 1941–1956). Alfred Harbage, *Shakespeare's Audience* (New York, 1941) throws light on the nature and tastes of the customers for whom Elizabethan dramatists wrote.

Although specialists disagree about details of stage construction, the reader will find essential information in John C. Adams, *The Globe Playhouse: Its Design and Equipment* (Barnes & Noble, 1961). A model of the Globe playhouse by Dr. Adams is on permanent exhibition in the Folger Shakespeare Library in Washington, D.C. An excellent description of the architecture of the Globe is Irwin Smith, *Shakespeare's Globe Playhouse: A Modern Reconstruction in Text and Scale Drawings Based upon the Reconstruction of the Globe*

by John Cranford Adams (New York, 1956). Another recent study of the physical characteristics of
the Globe is C. Walter Hodges, *The Globe Re-
stored* (London, 1953). An easily read history of
the early theatres is J. Q. Adams, *Shakespearean
Playhouses: A History of English Theatres from the
Beginnings to the Restoration* (Boston, 1917).

The following titles on theatrical history will provide information about Shakespeare's plays in later
periods: Alfred Harbage, *Theatre for Shakespeare*
(Toronto, 1955); Esther Cloudman Dunn, *Shakespeare in America* (New York, 1939); George C. D.
Odell, *Shakespeare from Betterton to Irving* (2 vols.,
London, 1921); Arthur Colby Sprague, *Shakespeare
and the Actors: The Stage Business in His Plays
(1660–1905)* (Cambridge, Mass., 1944) and *Shake-
spearian Players and Performances* (Cambridge,
Mass., 1953); Leslie Hotson, *The Commonwealth
and Restoration Stage* (Cambridge, Mass., 1928);
Alwin Thaler, *Shakspere to Sheridan: A Book About
the Theatre of Yesterday and To-day* (Cambridge,
Mass., 1922); Ernest Bradlee Watson, *Sheridan to
Robertson: A Study of the 19th-Century London
Stage* (Cambridge, Mass., 1926). Enid Welsford,
The Court Masque (Cambridge, Mass., 1927) is an
excellent study of the characteristics of this form
of entertainment.

The question of the authenticity of Shakespeare's
plays arouses perennial attention. A book that de-
molishes the notion of hidden cryptograms in the
plays is William F. Friedman and Elizebeth S.

Friedman, *The Shakespearean Ciphers Examined* (New York, 1957). A succinct account of the various absurdities advanced to suggest the authorship of a multitude of candidates other than Shakespeare will be found in R. C. Churchill, *Shakespeare and His Betters* (Bloomington, Ind., 1959) and Frank W. Wadsworth, *The Poacher from Stratford: A Partial Account of the Controversy over the Authorship of Shakespeare's Plays* (Berkeley, Calif., 1958). An essay on the curious notions in the writings of the anti-Shakespeareans is that by Louis B. Wright, "The Anti-Shakespeare Industry and the Growth of Cults," *The Virginia Quarterly Review,* XXXV (1959), 289–303.

Harley Granville-Barker, *Prefaces to Shakespeare* (5 vols., London, 1927–1948) provides stimulating critical discussion of the plays. An older classic of criticism is Andrew C. Bradley, *Shakespearean Tragedy: Lectures on Hamlet, Othello, King Lear, Macbeth* (London, 1904), which is now available in an inexpensive reprint (New York, 1955). Thomas M. Parrott, *Shakespearean Comedy* (New York, 1949) is scholarly and readable. Shakespeare's dramatizations of English history are examined in E. M. W. Tillyard, *Shakespeare's History Plays* (London, 1948), and Lily Bess Campbell, *Shakespeare's "Histories," Mirrors of Elizabethan Policy* (San Marino, Calif., 1947) contains a more technical discussion of the same subject.

Reprints of some of the sources of Shakespeare's plays can be found in *Shakespeare's Library* (2 vols., 1850), edited by John Payne Collier, and *The Shakespeare Classics* (12 vols., 1907–1926), edited by Israel Gollancz. Geoffrey Bullough, *Narrative and Dramatic Sources of Shakespeare* (New York, 1957) is a new series of volumes reprinting the sources. Two volumes covering the early comedies, comedies (1597–1603), and histories are now available. For discussion of Shakespeare's use of his sources see Kenneth Muir, *Shakespeare's Sources: Comedies and Tragedies* (London, 1957). Thomas M. Cranfill has recently edited a facsimile reprint of *Riche His Farewell to Military Profession* (1581), which contains stories that Shakespeare probably used for several of his plays. *The Famous Victories of Henry the Fifth* has been reprinted a number of times, and Samuel Daniel's *The Civil Wars* has been newly edited by Laurence Michel (New Haven, 1958).

More detailed information about *Henry IV, Part 1,* may be found in several recent editions of the play: Arthur R. Humphreys (ed.), *The First Part of the History of King Henry IV* (The Arden Shakespeare; London, 1960); S. B. Hemingway (ed.), *The New Variorum Edition of Shakespeare: Henry the Fourth, Part I* (Philadelphia, 1936); G. Blakemore Evans, *Supplement to the New Variorum Edition of Henry IV, Part I,* (*Shakespeare Quarterly,* VII, 3; New York, 1956); and John Dover Wilson (ed.), *The First Part of the History of Henry IV* (The New Cambridge Shakespeare; Cambridge, Eng., 1946).

For the historical background of *Henry IV,* James

H. Wylie, *The History of England under Henry the Fourth* (4 vols., London, 1884–1898), and the same author's *The Reign of Henry the Fifth* (3 vols., Cambridge, Eng., 1914–1929) will be useful. For the way in which Shakespeare used the material in Holinshed, see *Holinshed's Chronicle as Used in Shakespeare's Plays,* edited by Allardyce Nicoll and Josephine Nicoll (Everyman's Library; New York, 1951).

The vitality of Falstaff has inspired much commentary but the interested reader may find particularly significant Maurice Morgann, *An Essay on the Dramatic Character of Sir John Falstaff* (1777; reprinted in 1912). A more recent discussion of Falstaff will be found in the entertaining *Fortunes of Falstaff* by John Dover Wilson (Cambridge, Eng., 1943).

Interesting pictures as well as new information about Shakespeare will be found in F. E. Halliday, *Shakespeare, a Pictorial Biography* (London, 1956). Allardyce Nicoll, *The Elizabethans* (Cambridge, Eng., 1957) contains a variety of illustrations for the period.

A brief, clear, and accurate account of Tudor history is S. T. Bindoff, *The Tudors,* in the Penguin series. A readable general history is G. M. Trevelyan, *The History of England,* first published in 1926 and available in many editions. G. M. Trevelyan, *English Social History,* first published in 1942 and also available in many editions, provides fascinating information about England in all periods. Sir John Neale, *Queen Elizabeth* (London, 1934) is the best study of the great Queen. Various aspects of life in the Elizabethan period are treated in Louis B. Wright, *Middle-Class Culture in Eliza-bethan England* (Chapel Hill, N.C., 1935; reprinted by Cornell University Press, 1958). *Shakespeare's England: An Account of the Life and Manners of His Age*, edited by Sidney Lee and C. T. Onions (2 vols., Oxford, 1916) provides a large amount of information on many aspects of life in the Elizabethan period. Additional information will be found in Muriel St. C. Byrne, *Elizabethan Life in Town and Country* (Barnes & Noble, 1961).

The Folger Shakespeare Library is currently pub-lishing a series of illustrated pamphlets on various aspects of English life in the sixteenth and seven-teenth centuries. The following titles are available: Dorothy E. Mason, *Music in Elizabethan England;* Craig R. Thompson, *The English Church in the Six-teenth Century;* Louis B. Wright, *Shakespeare's Theatre and the Dramatic Tradition;* Giles E. Daw-son, *The Life of William Shakespeare;* Virginia A. LaMar, *English Dress in the Age of Shakespeare;* Craig R. Thompson, *The Bible in English, 1525–1611;* Craig R. Thompson, *Schools in Tudor Eng-land;* Craig R. Thompson, *Universities in Tudor England;* Lilly C. Stone, *English Sports and Recre-ations;* and Conyers Read, *The Government of Eng-land under Elizabeth.*

[Dramatis Personae.

King Henry the Fourth.
Henry, Prince of Wales,
Prince John of Lancaster, } sons to the King.
Earl of Westmoreland.
Sir Walter Blunt.
Thomas Percy, Earl of Worcester.
Henry Percy, Earl of Northumberland.
Henry Percy, nicknamed "Hotspur," son to the Earl of
    Northumberland.
Edmund Mortimer, Earl of March.
Richard Scroop, Archbishop of York.
Archibald, Earl of Douglas.
Owen Glendower.
Sir Richard Vernon.
Sir John Falstaff.
Sir Michael, friend to the Archbishop of York.
Poins.
Gadshill.
Peto.
Bardolph.
Vintner of the Boar's Head Tavern.
Francis, a drawer.
Chamberlain.
Ostler.

Lady Percy, wife to Hotspur.
Lady Mortimer, wife to Edmund Mortimer and daugh-
    ter to Glendower.
Mistress Quickly, hostess of the Boar's Head Tavern.

Sheriff, Carriers, Travelers, Messengers, Servants.

SCENE: England and Wales.]

THE HISTORY OF
HENRY
THE FOURTH
[PART 1]

ACT I

I. i. King Henry has called together his son John
and several of his trusted lords to discuss a crusade to
the Holy Land, long planned but delayed by civil
tumult. He learns, however, of new hostilities by the
Scots. Henry Percy, son of the Earl of Northumberland, has defeated the Douglas but has refused to re-
linquish his prisoners to the King. The King is grieved
to hear of the engagement for two reasons: the valiant deeds of young Percy, nicknamed "Hotspur,"
contrast painfully with the idle life pursued by his
own son Henry, and the retention of prisoners promises to cause strife with Northumberland. Until the
question of the prisoners is resolved, plans for the
crusade will have to be postponed.

<hr/>

**2-3. pant/And breathe short-winded accents
of new broils:** catch her breath and gasp out word
of new wars.

4. stronds: strands; shores.

**5-6. No more the thirsty entrance of this soil/
Shall daub her lips with her own children's
blood:** no longer shall the absorbent earth of this
country be smeared with the blood of her people.

7. trenching: gashing.

**10-1. like the meteors of a troubled heaven,/
All of one nature, of one substance bred:** meteors
were believed to be exhalations of gas from the heavenly bodies. They are, consequently, here compared
to the offspring of the **troubled heaven** just as the
opposed eyes are all the offspring of the same par-
ent—England.

12. intestine: internal; domestic.

13. close: grapple.

14. mutual well-beseeming ranks: united and
orderly ranks.

18. his: its.

ACT I

Scene I. [London. The palace.]

Enter the *King, Lord John of Lancaster, Earl of Westmoreland,* [*Sir Walter Blunt,*] with *others.*

King. So shaken as we are, so wan with care,
Find we a time for frighted peace to pant
And breathe short-winded accents of new broils
To be commenced in stronds afar remote.
No more the thirsty entrance of this soil   5
Shall daub her lips with her own children's blood:
No more shall trenching war channel her fields,
Nor bruise her flow'rets with the armed hoofs
Of hostile paces. Those opposed eyes
Which, like the meteors of a troubled heaven,   10
All of one nature, of one substance bred,
Did lately meet in the intestine shock
And furious close of civil butchery,
Shall now in mutual well-beseeming ranks
March all one way and be no more opposed   15
Against acquaintance, kindred, and allies.
The edge of war, like an ill-sheathed knife,
No more shall cut his master. Therefore, friends,
As far as to the sepulcher of Christ—

21. **impressed:** enlisted; **engaged:** pledged.

29. **bootless:** in vain; useless.

30. **Therefor:** for that purpose; namely, to set forth on the crusade.

31. **cousin:** the King and the Earl were not cousins in the precise modern sense but were related only by marriage. The word **cousin** was used as a vague term of kinship.

33. **dear expedience:** important and urgent undertaking.

34. **this haste was hot in question:** this urgent matter was earnestly discussed.

35. **limits of the charge:** divisions of responsibility.

36. **all athwart:** completely thwarting our plans.

37. **post:** messenger, riding at utmost speed; **heavy:** grave.

38. **Mortimer:** Sir Edmund Mortimer.

40. **irregular:** guerrilla.

43. **corpse:** i.e., corpses; those of the thousand, not the corpse of Mortimer.

Whose soldier now, under whose blessed cross　　　20
We are impressed and engaged to fight—
Forthwith a power of English shall we levy,
Whose arms were molded in their mother's womb
To chase these pagans in those holy fields
Over whose acres walked those blessed feet　　　25
Which fourteen hundred years ago were nailed
For our advantage on the bitter cross.
But this our purpose now is twelve month old,
And bootless 'tis to tell you we will go.
Therefor we meet not now. Then let me hear　　　30
Of you, my gentle cousin Westmoreland,
What yesternight our council did decree
In forwarding this dear expedience.

West. My liege, this haste was hot in question
And many limits of the charge set down　　　35
But yesternight; when all athwart there came
A post from Wales, loaden with heavy news,
Whose worst was that the noble Mortimer,
Leading the men of Herefordshire to fight
Against the irregular and wild Glendower,　　　40
Was by the rude hands of that Welshman taken,
A thousand of his people butchered;
Upon whose dead corpse there was such misuse,
Such beastly shameless transformation,
By those Welshwomen done as may not be　　　45
Without much shame retold or spoken of.

King. It seems then that the tidings of this broil
Brake off our business for the Holy Land.

West. This, matched with other, did, my gracious
　　lord;　　　50

51. **uneven:** disturbing.

53. **Holy-rood Day:** September 14.

55. **ever-valiant and approved:** i.e., whose habitual valor has been demonstrated by trial.

56. **Holmedon:** Humbleton, Northumberland.

58-9. **by discharge of their artillery/And shape of likelihood:** that is, by the sound of their cannon, which made heavy losses seem likely.

60. **them: the news,** often used in the plural in accordance with its derivation from the Latin *res novae* (new things); **in the very heat/And pride:** at the height of the battle.

70. **Balked in their own blood: a balk** is a mound or ridge and, as a verb, means to disappoint or frustrate (by having an obstacle in the way). Hence as Shakespeare uses it here **balked** can mean both "piled up in heaps" and "stopped in their course"—defeated.

72. **Mordake, Earl of Fife:** Shakespeare was mistaken in calling **Mordake** (Murdoch) eldest son to the Douglas, having misinterpreted a passage in Holinshed. In reality, Murdoch was the Duke of Albany's son.

74. **Menteith:** another error taken from Holinshed. Earl of Menteith was another of Murdoch's titles, not a different man.

For more uneven and unwelcome news
Came from the North, and thus it did import:
On Holy-rood Day the gallant Hotspur there,
Young Harry Percy, and brave Archibald,
That ever-valiant and approved Scot,   55
At Holmedon met, where they did spend
A sad and bloody hour;
As by discharge of their artillery
And shape of likelihood the news was told;
For he that brought them, in the very heat   60
And pride of their contention did take horse,
Uncertain of the issue any way.
    King. Here is a dear, a true industrious friend,
Sir Walter Blunt, new lighted from his horse,
Stained with the variation of each soil   65
Betwixt that Holmedon and this seat of ours,
And he hath brought us smooth and welcome news.
The Earl of Douglas is discomfited;
Ten thousand bold Scots, two-and-twenty knights,
Balked in their own blood did Sir Walter see   70
On Holmedon's plains. Of prisoners, Hotspur took
Mordake, Earl of Fife, and eldest son
To beaten Douglas, and the Earl of Athol,
Of Murray, Angus, and Menteith.
And is not this an honorable spoil?   75
A gallant prize? Ha, cousin, is it not?
    West. In faith,
It is a conquest for a prince to boast of.
    King. Yea, there thou makest me sad, and makest
        me sin   80
In envy that my Lord Northumberland

85. **minion:** darling.

88-92. **O . . . mine:** for dramatic effect, Shakespeare portrays Hotspur and Prince Henry as near in age and the King as older than, in fact, he was. Harry Hotspur was actually a little older than the King and twenty-three years older than the Prince.

93. **let him from my thoughts:** i.e., let me forget him.

95. **surprised:** taken as prizes.

96. **To his own use:** for the profit he could gain by ransoming them.

99. **Malevolent to you in all aspects: aspects** is used in an astrological sense meaning the relative position of the planets as they appear on the earth at a given time. The meaning is that Worcester is the King's enemy, any way you look at him.

100.. **prune:** preen, as a bird of prey does before an encounter. **Him** refers to Hotspur, not Worcester.

Should be the father to so blest a son—
A son who is the theme of honor's tongue,
Amongst a grove the very straightest plant;
Who is sweet Fortune's minion and her pride;   85
Whilst I, by looking on the praise of him,
See riot and dishonor stain the brow
Of my young Harry. O that it could be proved
That some night-tripping fairy had exchanged
In cradle clothes our children where they lay,   90
And called mine Percy, his Plantagenet!
Then would I have his Harry, and he mine.
But let him from my thoughts. What think you, coz,
Of this young Percy's pride? The prisoners
Which he in this adventure hath surprised   95
To his own use he keeps, and sends me word
I shall have none but Mordake, Earl of Fife.

West. This is his uncle's teaching, this is Worcester,
Malevolent to you in all aspects,
Which makes him prune himself and bristle up   100
The crest of youth against your dignity.

King. But I have sent for him to answer this;
And for this cause awhile we must neglect
Our holy purpose to Jerusalem.
Cousin, on Wednesday next our council we   105
Will hold at Windsor. So inform the lords;
But come yourself with speed to us again;
For more is to be said and to be done
Than out of anger can be uttered.

    West. I will, my liege.   110

                        Exeunt.

I. ii. Prince Henry is portrayed as the companion of a group of merry rogues. He is matching wits with Sir John Falstaff when Poins, a confederate, reports the plan for a robbery arranged by Gadshill, a professional thief. The Prince declines to take part, but Poins urges him to pretend to do so in order that they may play a trick on Falstaff. The Prince and Poins agree to disguise themselves and rob Falstaff and the other members of the band of the booty they plan to take from the travelers whom Gadshill has spotted as their victims. It will be great sport to hear Falstaff's tale of his own valor in coping with the assault of a rival band of thieves. In an aside, the Prince explains his behavior: he is wearing a deliberate mask of frivolity which he will throw off when the time is ripe for him to show his real seriousness. His reformation will seem all the more striking because it will be so unexpected.

2. **old:** old sometimes has the meaning "excessive" and Shakespeare may be using it in two senses here.

3. **sack:** sherry.

9. **leaping houses:** brothels.

13. **come near me now:** hit me close to home.

14. **seven stars:** Pleiades.

15. **Phoebus:** the sun; **that wand'ring knight:** Falstaff thinks of the hero of a popular romance, either The Knight of the Sun in a romance translated from Spanish as *The Mirror of Knighthood* (1578?), or *The Wandering Knight,* translated from the French of Jean Cartigny in 1581.

20. **troth:** faith.

22. **roundly:** plainly; tell me straight out what you mean.

23. **Marry:** indeed; originally an oath "By the Virgin Mary."

25-6. **Diana's foresters:** Diana was the virgin huntress as well as goddess of the moon.

5

Scene II. [London. An apartment of Prince Henry.]

Enter *Prince of Wales* and *Sir John Falstaff*.

Fal. Now, Hal, what time of day is it, lad?

Prince. Thou art so fat-witted with drinking of old
sack, and unbuttoning thee after supper, and sleep-
ing upon benches after noon, that thou hast forgotten
to demand that truly which thou wouldst truly know.   5
What a devil hast thou to do with the time of the
day? Unless hours were cups of sack, and minutes
capons, and clocks the tongues of bawds, and dials
the signs of leaping houses, and the blessed sun himself a fair hot wench in flame-colored taffeta, I see no   10
reason why thou shouldst be so superfluous to demand the time of the day.

Fal. Indeed you come near me now, Hal; for we
that take purses go by the moon and the seven stars,
and not by Phoebus, he, that wand'ring knight so   15
fair. And I prithee, sweet wag, when thou art a king,
as, God save thy Grace—Majesty I should say, for
grace thou wilt have none—

Prince. What, none?

Fal. No, by my troth; not so much as will serve to   20
be prologue to an egg and butter.

Prince. Well, how then? Come, roundly, roundly.

Fal. Marry, then, sweet wag, when thou art King,
let not us that are squires of the night's body be
called thieves of the day's beauty. Let us be Diana's   25
foresters, gentlemen of the shade, minions of the

27-8. **of good government:** i.e., well-controlled.

29. **countenance:** two meanings: "face" and "approval."

31. **it holds well too:** i.e., your metaphor is also apt.

36-7. **swearing "Lay by":** a bandit's demand for a traveler's goods, with curses for emphasis; **"Bring in":** the command to bring drink in a tavern.

38. **ladder:** the one leading to the gallows.

42-3. **Hybla:** Mount Hybla in Sicily produced honey famed for its flavor; **old lad of the castle:** in the play as first written by Shakespeare, Falstaff was named Sir John Oldcastle, but a historical personage bore this name and Shakespeare later changed it to Falstaff. This allusion may show carelessness in revision, but the term also means a noisy reveler.

43. **buff jerkin:** a leather coat of the type worn by sheriff's officers.

44. **durance:** a durable cloth, with a pun referring to imprisonment.

50. **reckoning:** tavern account.

moon; and let men say we be men of good government, being governed as the sea is, by our noble and
chaste mistress the moon, under whose countenance
we steal.　　30

Prince. Thou sayest well, and it holds well too; for
the fortune of us that are the moon's men doth ebb
and flow like the sea, being governed, as the sea is,
by the moon. As, for proof now: a purse of gold most
resolutely snatched on Monday night and most disso-　35
lutely spent on Tuesday morning; got with swearing
"Lay by," and spent with crying "Bring in"; now in as
low an ebb as the foot of the ladder, and by and by
in as high a flow as the ridge of the gallows.

Fal. By the Lord, thou sayst true, lad—and is not　40
my hostess of the tavern a most sweet wench?

Prince. As the honey of Hybla, my old lad of the
castle—and is not a buff jerkin a most sweet robe of
durance?

Fal. How now, how now, mad wag? What, in thy　45
quips and thy quiddities? What a plague have I to
do with a buff jerkin?

Prince. Why, what a pox have I to do with my
hostess of the tavern?

Fal. Well, thou hast called her to a reckoning many　50
a time and oft.

Prince. Did I ever call for thee to pay thy part?

Fal. No; I'll give thee thy due, thou hast paid all
there.

Prince. Yea, and elsewhere, so far as my coin would　55
stretch; and where it would not, I have used my
credit.

61. **resolution:** determination to steal; **fubbed:** baffled.

62. **antic:** buffoon.

65. **brave:** splendid.

70. **in some sort:** in a way; to a degree; **jumps:** agrees.

75. **'Sblood:** by God's blood.

76. **gib-cat:** tomcat. Gib (a nickname for Gilbert) was a common name for a cat; **lugged:** baited. Bear-baiting with mastiffs was a popular sport.

79. **hare:** proverbially a melancholy animal.

80. **Moor Ditch:** a sewer outside the city walls into which the marshy Moorfields drained.

82. **comparative:** quick at uncomplimentary comparisons.

84. **vanity:** foolishness.

85. **commodity:** quantity.

86. **rated:** berated; scolded.

Fal. Yea, and so used it that, were it not here apparent that thou art heir apparent—But I prithee, sweet wag, shall there be gallows standing in England when thou art King? and resolution thus fubbed as it is with the rusty curb of old father antic the law? Do not thou, when thou art King, hang a thief.

Prince. No; thou shalt.

Fal. Shall I? O rare! By the Lord, I'll be a brave judge.

Prince. Thou judgest false already. I mean, thou shalt have the hanging of the thieves and so become a rare hangman.

Fal. Well, Hal, well; and in some sort it jumps with my humor as well as waiting in the court, I can tell you.

Prince. For obtaining of suits?

Fal. Yea, for obtaining of suits, whereof the hangman hath no lean wardrobe. 'Sblood, I am as melancholy as a gib-cat or a lugged bear.

Prince. Or an old lion, or a lover's lute.

Fal. Yea, or the drone of a Lincolnshire bagpipe.

Prince. What sayest thou to a hare, or the melancholy of Moor Ditch?

Fal. Thou hast the most unsavory similes, and art indeed the most comparative, rascalliest, sweet young prince. But, Hal, I prithee trouble me no more with vanity. I would to God thou and I knew where a commodity of good names were to be bought. An old lord of the council rated me the other day in the street about you, sir, but I marked him not; and yet

90-1. **wisdom cries out in the streets, and no man regards it:** Proverbs 1:20-4: "Wisdom crieth without; she uttereth her voice in the streets. She crieth . . . I have called and ye refused; I have stretched out my hand and no man regarded."

92. **damnable iteration:** abominable repetition. The Prince has outwitted Falstaff by capping his Scriptural allusion with a more exact quotation; in return Falstaff implies that the Devil can quote Scripture.

95. **knew nothing:** i.e., was innocent and unsophisticated.

98. **an:** if.

102. **Zounds:** by God's wounds; **make one:** join your party; go along.

103. **villain:** low fellow; **baffle:** degrade; disgrace.

108-9. **Gadshill:** the reader should remember to distinguish the man named Gadshill here and the place Gad's Hill mentioned below, a notorious resort of highwaymen; **set a match:** set up a robbery; **by merit:** i.e., instead of by Divine Grace.

111. **omnipotent:** unparalleled.

112. **true:** honest.

115. **Sack and Sugar:** sack was often sweetened with a bit of sugar.

he talked very wisely, but I regarded him not; and
yet he talked wisely, and in the street too.

Prince. Thou didst well, for wisdom cries out in   90
the streets, and no man regards it.

Fal. O, thou hast damnable iteration, and art indeed able to corrupt a saint. Thou hast done much
harm upon me, Hal, God forgive thee for it! Before
I knew thee, Hal, I knew nothing; and now am I, if   95
a man should speak truly, little better than one of the
wicked. I must give over this life, and I will give it
over! By the Lord, an I do not, I am a villain! I'll be
damned for never a king's son in Christendom.

Prince. Where shall we take a purse tomorrow,   100
Jack?

Fal. Zounds, where thou wilt, lad! I'll make one.
An I do not, call me villain and baffle me.

Prince. I see a good amendment of life in thee—
from praying to purse-taking.   105

Fal. Why, Hal, 'tis my vocation, Hal. 'Tis no sin
for a man to labor in his vocation.

Enter *Poins.*

Poins! Now shall we know if Gadshill have set a
match. O, if men were to be saved by merit, what
hole in hell were hot enough for him? This is the   110
most omnipotent villain that ever cried "Stand!" to a
true man.

Prince. Good morrow, Ned.

Poins. Good morrow, sweet Hal. What says Mon-
sieur Remorse? What says Sir John Sack and Sugar?   115

124. **cozening:** cheating.

129-30. **vizards:** masks.

131. **bespoke:** ordered.

132. **Eastcheap:** a section of London where the Boar's Head Tavern was located.

136. **Yedward:** Edward.

138. **chops:** fat-jaws; fat-face.

141. **honesty:** honor.

143. **royal:** a coin worth ten shillings. Falstaff is punning.

Jack, how agrees the Devil and thee about thy soul, that thou soldest him on Good Friday last for a cup of Madeira and a cold capon's leg?

Prince. Sir John stands to his word, the Devil shall have his bargain; for he was never yet a breaker of proverbs. He will give the Devil his due. 120

Poins. Then art thou damned for keeping thy word with the Devil.

Prince. Else he had been damned for cozening the Devil. 125

Poins. But, my lads, my lads, tomorrow morning, by four o'clock early, at Gad's Hill! There are pilgrims going to Canterbury with rich offerings, and traders riding to London with fat purses. I have vizards for you all; you have horses for yourselves. Gadshill lies tonight in Rochester. I have bespoke supper tomorrow night in Eastcheap. We may do it as secure as sleep. If you will go, I will stuff your purses full of crowns; if you will not, tarry at home and be hanged! 130 135

Fal. Hear ye, Yedward: if I tarry at home and go not, I'll hang you for going.

Poins. You will, chops?

Fal. Hal, wilt thou make one?

Prince. Who, I rob? I a thief? Not I, by my faith. 140

Fal. There's neither honesty, manhood, nor good fellowship in thee, nor thou camest not of the blood royal if thou darest not stand for ten shillings.

Prince. Well then, once in my days I'll be a madcap. 145

Fal. Why, that's well said.

158. **want:** lack.

159. **countenance:** approval; see l. 29.

161. **thou latter spring:** that is, you young-old man, an idea repeated in **All-hallown summer.** All Hallow's Day falls on November 1.

177. **like:** likely.

Prince. Well, come what will, I'll tarry at home.

Fal. By the Lord, I'll be a traitor then, when thou art King.

Prince. I care not.   150

Poins. Sir John, I prithee, leave the Prince and me alone. I will lay him down such reasons for this adventure that he shall go.

Fal. Well, God give thee the spirit of persuasion and him the ears of profiting, that what thou speak- 155
est may move and what he hears may be believed, that the true Prince may (for recreation sake) prove a false thief; for the poor abuses of the time want countenance. Farewell; you shall find me in East-cheap.   160

Prince. Farewell, thou latter spring! farewell, All-hallown summer!   [*Exit Falstaff.*]

Poins. Now, my good sweet honey lord, ride with us tomorrow. I have a jest to execute that I cannot manage alone. Falstaff, Bardolph, Peto, and Gadshill 165
shall rob those men that we have already waylaid; yourself and I will not be there; and when they have the booty, if you and I do not rob them, cut this head off from my shoulders.

Prince. How shall we part with them in setting 170
forth?

Poins. Why, we will set forth before or after them and appoint them a place of meeting, wherein it is at our pleasure to fail; and then will they adventure upon the exploit themselves, which they shall have 175
no sooner achieved, but we'll set upon them.

Prince. Yea, but 'tis like that they will know us by

178-79. **habits:** apparel; **appointment:** equipment.

182. **cases:** suits; **buckram:** a kind of coarse and stiff linen cloth.

183. **nonce:** occasion; i.e., for that specific need; **noted:** known.

185. **doubt:** fear.

190-91. **incomprehensible:** inconceivable.

193. **wards:** defenses.

194: **reproof:** disproof.

200-1. **uphold/The unyoked humor of your idleness:** maintain your unchecked course of folly.

203. **contagious:** disease-breeding. Clouds were believed to carry infection.

our horses, by our habits, and by every other appointment, to be ourselves.

Poins. Tut! our horses they shall not see—I'll tie 180
them in the wood; our vizards we will change after
we leave them; and, sirrah, I have cases of buckram
for the nonce, to immask our noted outward garments.

Prince. Yea, but I doubt they will be too hard for 185
us.

Poins. Well, for two of them, I know them to be
as true-bred cowards as ever turned back; and for the
third, if he fight longer than he sees reason, I'll for-
swear arms. The virtue of this jest will be the incom- 190
prehensible lies that this same fat rogue will tell us
when we meet at supper: how thirty, at least, he
fought with; what wards, what blows, what extremi-
ties he endured; and in the reproof of this lives the
jest. 195

Prince. Well, I'll go with thee. Provide us all things
necessary and meet me tonight in Eastcheap. There
I'll sup. Farewell.

Poins. Farewell, my lord. *Exit.*

Prince. I know you all, and will awhile uphold 200
The unyoked humor of your idleness.
Yet herein will I imitate the sun,
Who doth permit the base contagious clouds
To smother up his beauty from the world,
That, when he please again to be himself, 205
Being wanted, he may be more wond'red at
By breaking through the foul and ugly mists
Of vapors that did seem to strangle him.

212. **rare accidents:** happenings that are infrequent and therefore more highly prized.

216. **hopes:** expectations.

217. **sullen:** dull.

221. **skill:** cunning stratagem.

222. **Redeeming time:** reclaiming (making good) the time I have lost.

◼◼◼◼◼◼◼◼◼◼◼◼◼◼◼◼◼◼◼◼◼◼◼◼◼◼◼◼◼◼◼

I. iii. The King meets with Northumberland, Hotspur, and Worcester to settle the matter of the prisoners. Hotspur explains the circumstances of his original refusal, but still declines to surrender the men unless the King will ransom Mortimer, who is prisoner of the Welsh leader, Owen Glendower. The King's view is that Mortimer voluntarily joined the Welsh rebels, and he refuses to buy a traitor. He threatens the Percies with dire consequences if they do not hand over the prisoners.

Hotspur is enraged at the King's attitude and resolves to defy him. His father and uncle are equally rebellious at what they consider the King's ingratitude for their past support, and they plan a league with the Scots, Welsh, and other groups hostile to King Henry.

◼◼◼◼◼◼◼◼◼◼◼◼◼◼◼◼◼◼◼◼◼◼◼◼◼◼◼

3. **found me:** i.e., noticed this characteristic of mine.

5-6. **rather be myself . . . than my condition:** rather be the King than act according to my temperament.

If all the year were playing holidays,
To sport would be as tedious as to work;   210
But when they seldom come, they wished-for come,
And nothing pleaseth but rare accidents.
So, when this loose behavior I throw off
And pay the debt I never promised,
By how much better than my word I am,   215
By so much shall I falsify men's hopes;
And, like bright metal on a sullen ground,
My reformation, glitt'ring o'er my fault,
Shall show more goodly and attract more eyes
Than that which hath no foil to set it off.   220
I'll so offend to make offense a skill,
Redeeming time when men think least I will.

                                        Exit.

Scene III. [Windsor Castle.]

Enter the King, Northumberland, Worcester,
Hotspur, Sir Walter Blunt, *with* others.

  King. My blood hath been too cold and temperate,
Unapt to stir at these indignities,
And you have found me, for accordingly
You tread upon my patience; but be sure
I will from henceforth rather be myself,   5
Mighty and to be feared, than my condition,
Which hath been smooth as oil, soft as young down,
And therefore lost that title of respect
Which the proud soul ne'er pays but to the proud.

13. **holp:** helped; **portly:** majestic.

16. **Danger:** rebellion.

17. **presence:** carriage; **peremptory:** imperious.

19. **The moody frontier of a servant brow:** i.e., a frown on an inferior's forehead.

20. **good leave:** full permission.

27. **delivered:** reported.

28. **envy . . . or misprision:** malice or distorted report.

37. **milliner:** that is, a tradesman who dealt in hats and gloves and other finery—not a woman.

39. **pouncet box:** small container which held a perfumed mixture. Men and women alike used them to counteract unpleasant odors and protect against infection.

Wor. Our house, my sovereign liege, little deserves　10
The scourge of greatness to be used on it—
And that same greatness too which our own hands
Have holp to make so portly.

　North. My lord—

　King. Worcester, get thee gone, for I do see　15
Danger and disobedience in thine eye.
O sir, your presence is too bold and peremptory,
And majesty might never yet endure
The moody frontier of a servant brow.
You have good leave to leave us: when we need　20
Your use and counsel, we shall send for you.

　　　　　　　　　　　　　Exit Worcester.

You were about to speak.

　North.　　　　　　　Yea, my good lord.
Those prisoners in your Highness' name demanded
Which Harry Percy here at Holmedon took,　25
Were, as he says, not with such strength denied
As is delivered to your Majesty.
Either envy, therefore, or misprision
Is guilty of this fault, and not my son.

　Hot. My liege, I did deny no prisoners.　30
But I remember, when the fight was done,
When I was dry with rage and extreme toil,
Breathless and faint, leaning upon my sword,
Came there a certain lord, neat and trimly dressed,
Fresh as a bridegroom, and his chin new reaped　35
Showed like a stubble land at harvest home.
He was perfumed like a milliner,
And 'twixt his finger and his thumb he held
A pouncet box, which ever and anon

42. **Took it in snuff:** inhaled it quickly and angrily (because of having been deprived). The phrase to take something "in snuff" meant to show anger or resentment. **Who** refers to his nose; **still:** constantly.

51. **popinjay:** showy bird.

53. **neglectingly:** negligently; thoughtlessly.

57-8. **God save the mark:** usually uttered to avert trouble at mention of catastrophe. Here the meaning is something akin to "Heaven preserve us from such a fellow's meddling in martial matters."

59. **sovereignest:** strongest in curative power.

60. **parmacity:** a waxy substance from the head of a sperm whale, used in ointments.

64. **tall:** brave.

67. **bald:** meaningless.

68. **indirectly:** evasively.

70. **Come current:** that is, be credited.

He gave his nose, and took't away again;   40
Who therewith angry, when it next came there,
Took it in snuff; and still he smiled and talked;
And as the soldiers bore dead bodies by,
He called them untaught knaves, unmannerly,
To bring a slovenly unhandsome corse   45
Betwixt the wind and his nobility.
With many holiday and lady terms
He questioned me, amongst the rest demanded
My prisoners in your Majesty's behalf.
I then, all smarting with my wounds being cold,   50
To be so pestered with a popinjay,
Out of my grief and my impatience
Answered neglectingly, I know not what—
He should, or he should not; for he made me mad
To see him shine so brisk, and smell so sweet,   55
And talk so like a waiting gentlewoman
Of guns and drums and wounds—God save the
    mark!—
And telling me the sovereignest thing on earth
Was parmacity for an inward bruise,   60
And that it was great pity, so it was,
This villainous saltpeter should be digged
Out of the bowels of the harmless earth,
Which many a good tall fellow had destroyed
So cowardly, and but for these vile guns,   65
He would himself have been a soldier.
This bald unjointed chat of his, my lord,
I answered indirectly, as I said,
And I beseech you, let not his report
Come current for an accusation   70

77. **impeach:** accuse; that is, task with wrong-doing.

81. **straight:** immediately.

82. **brother-in-law . . . Mortimer:** Shakespeare has confused Sir Edmund Mortimer, the Mortimer captured by Glendower, with his nephew, Edmund Mortimer, Earl of March. Hotspur was married to Sir Edmund's sister Elizabeth, whose brother, Roger, 4th Earl of March, had been recognized by Richard II as heir to his throne. At the time of the Percy conspiracy, Roger was dead and his son Edmund, current holder of the title Earl of March, was regarded by many as the claimant with the strongest right to the throne.

89. **indent with fears:** make an agreement with persons who threaten our safety. **Indent** (short for "indenture") is a legal term.

96. **fall off:** desert your party.

99. **mouthed:** gaping. Shakespeare often pictures wounds as having mouths, and here the word **mouthed** carries on the metaphor of the **tongue** defending Mortimer.

Betwixt my love and your high Majesty.

Blunt. The circumstance considered, good my lord,
Whate'er Lord Harry Percy then had said
To such a person, and in such a place,
At such a time, with all the rest retold,   75
May reasonably die, and never rise
To do him wrong, or any way impeach
What then he said, so he unsay it now.

King. Why, yet he doth deny his prisoners,
But with proviso and exception,   80
That we at our own charge shall ransom straight
His brother-in-law, the foolish Mortimer;
Who, on my soul, hath willfully betrayed
The lives of those that he did lead to fight
Against that great magician, damned Glendower,   85
Whose daughter, as we hear, that Earl of March
Hath lately married. Shall our coffers, then,
Be emptied to redeem a traitor home?
Shall we buy treason? and indent with fears
When they have lost and forfeited themselves?   90
No, on the barren mountains let him starve!
For I shall never hold that man my friend
Whose tongue shall ask me for one penny cost
To ransom home revolted Mortimer.

Hot. Revolted Mortimer?   95
He never did fall off, my sovereign liege,
But by the chance of war. To prove that true
Needs no more but one tongue for all those wounds,
Those mouthed wounds, which valiantly he took
When on the gentle Severn's sedgy bank,   100
In single opposition hand to hand,

102. **confound:** use up.

103. **changing hardiment:** exchanging valiant blows; fighting hand to hand.

104. **breathed:** i.e., took a breather.

109. **his:** its; **crisp:** curled; rippled.

111-12. **Never did bare and rotten policy/ Color her working with such deadly wounds:** Hotspur points out that Mortimer need not have fought so fiercely to disguise his treachery. **Policy** is equivalent to political treachery.

115. **with revolt:** that is, with the accusation of disloyalty.

116. **belie:** lie about.

129. **An if:** if.

He did confound the best part of an hour
In changing hardiment with great Glendower.
Three times they breathed, and three times did they
        drink,   105
Upon agreement, of swift Severn's flood;
Who then, affrighted with their bloody looks,
Ran fearfully among the trembling reeds
And hid his crisp head in the hollow bank,
Bloodstained with these valiant combatants.   110
Never did bare and rotten policy
Color her working with such deadly wounds;
Nor never could the noble Mortimer
Receive so many, and all willingly.
Then let not him be slandered with revolt.   115
    King. Thou dost belie him, Percy, thou dost belie
        him!
He never did encounter with Glendower.
I tell thee
He durst as well have met the Devil alone   120
As Owen Glendower for an enemy.
Art thou not ashamed? But, sirrah, henceforth
Let me not hear you speak of Mortimer.
Send me your prisoners with the speediest means,
Or you shall hear in such a kind from me   125
As will displease you. My Lord Northumberland,
We license your departure with your son.—
Send us your prisoners, or you will hear of it.
                    Exeunt King, [Blunt, and train].
    Hot. An if the Devil come and roar for them,
I will not send them. I will after straight   130
And tell him so; for I will ease my heart,

132. **hazard:** pawn.

133. **choler:** anger.

139. **on his part:** for his cause.

143. **cankered:** ulcerated; eaten by resentment and envy; **Bolingbroke:** King Henry IV was originally called Henry Bolingbroke, from the place of his birth. Percy is remembering that Henry did not always have the right to the throne.

147. **forsooth:** truly—"If you can believe it."

148. **urged:** mentioned.

150. **eye of death:** eye betraying mortal fear.

156. **in us:** i.e., done by us.

Albeit I make a hazard of my head.
　North. What, drunk with choler? Stay, and pause
　　awhile.
Here comes your uncle.　　　　　　　　　　135

　　　　　　[Re-]enter *Worcester.*

　Hot.　　　　　　Speak of Mortimer?
Zounds, I will speak of him, and let my soul
Want mercy if I do not join with him!
Yea, on his part I'll empty all these veins,
And shed my dear blood drop by drop in the dust,　140
But I will lift the downtrod Mortimer
As high in the air as this unthankful King,
As this ingrate and cankered Bolingbroke.
　North. Brother, the King hath made your nephew
　　mad.　　　　　　　　　　　　　　145
　Wor. Who struck this heat up after I was gone?
　Hot. He will (forsooth) have all my prisoners;
And when I urged the ransom once again
Of my wive's brother, then his cheek looked pale,
And on my face he turned an eye of death,　150
Trembling even at the name of Mortimer.
　Wor. I cannot blame him. Was not he proclaimed
By Richard that dead is the next of blood?
　North. He was; I heard the proclamation.
And then it was when the unhappy King　155
(Whose wrongs in us God pardon!) did set forth
Upon his Irish expedition;
From whence he intercepted did return
To be deposed, and shortly murdered.

164. **brother:** brother-in-law. See explanation of Shakespeare's confusion of the Mortimers at l. 82.

172. **murderous subornation:** incitement to murder.

177-78. **the line and the predicament/Wherein you range:** i.e., exactly where you stand. **Predicament** means position.

182. **gage:** pledge.

185. **canker:** canker or dog rose; a wild variety.

Wor. And for whose death we in the world's wide 160
    mouth
Live scandalized and foully spoken of.
  Hot. But soft, I pray you. Did King Richard then
Proclaim my brother Edmund Mortimer
Heir to the crown?   165
  North.   He did; myself did hear it.
  Hot. Nay, then I cannot blame his cousin King,
That wished him on the barren mountains starve.
But shall it be that you, that set the crown
Upon the head of this forgetful man,   170
And for his sake wear the detested blot
Of murderous subornation—shall it be
That you a world of curses undergo,
Being the agents or base second means,
The cords, the ladder, or the hangman rather?   175
O pardon me that I descend so low
To show the line and the predicament
Wherein you range under this subtle King!
Shall it for shame be spoken in these days,
Or fill up chronicles in time to come,   180
That men of your nobility and power
Did gage them both in an unjust behalf
(As both of you, God pardon it! have done)
To put down Richard, that sweet lovely rose,
And plant this thorn, this canker, Bolingbroke?   185
And shall it in more shame be further spoken
That you are fooled, discarded, and shook off
By him for whom these shames ye underwent?
No! yet time serves wherein you may redeem
Your banished honors and restore yourselves   190

192. **disdained:** disdainful.

194. **answer:** repay.

199. **quick-conceiving discontents:** that is, Hotspur's discontented mind will enable him to grasp Worcester's meaning quickly.

210. **patience:** restraint; moderation.

211. **were:** would be.

214. **fathom line:** a line to measure depth.

217. **corrival:** partner.

218. **out upon this half-faced fellowship:** away with inferior companionship in the pursuit of honor. Hotspur disdains the idea that anyone can rival his zeal in daring all hazards for honor's sake and would prefer not to share any of the glory.

219. **apprehends:** conceives; **figures:** images.

220. **form:** i.e., the exact detail; **attend:** heed.

221. **give me audience:** listen to me.

Into the good thoughts of the world again;
Revenge the jeering and disdained contempt
Of this proud King, who' studies day and night
To answer all the debt he owes to you
Even with the bloody payment of your deaths.   195
Therefore I say—
  Wor.   Peace, cousin, say no more;
And now I will unclasp a secret book,
And to your quick-conceiving discontents
I'll read you matter deep and dangerous,   200
As full of peril and adventurous spirit
As to o'erwalk a current roaring loud
On the unsteadfast footing of a spear.
  Hot. If he fall in, good night, or sink or swim!
Send danger from the east unto the west,   205
So honor cross it from the north to south,
And let them grapple. O, the blood more stirs
To rouse a lion than to start a hare!
  North. Imagination of some great exploit
Drives him beyond the bounds of patience.   210
  Hot. By heaven, methinks it were an easy leap
To pluck bright honor from the pale-faced moon,
Or dive into the bottom of the deep,
Where fathom line could never touch the ground,
And pluck up drowned honor by the locks,   215
So he that doth redeem her thence might wear
Without corrival all her dignities;
But out upon this half-faced fellowship!
  Wor. He apprehends a world of figures here,
But not the form of what he should attend.   220
Good cousin, give me audience for a while.

222. **cry you mercy:** beg your pardon.

228. **by this hand:** an oath.

239. **still:** continually; see l. 42.

241. **studies:** preoccupations; **defy:** reject.

242. **gall:** irritate; annoy.

243. **sword-and-buckler:** a combination of short sword and buckler (shield) was the equipment of apprentices and servingmen and not the weapons of a gentleman. Hotspur compares the Prince to a vulgar brawler in the street.

Hot. I cry you mercy.

Wor.   Those same noble Scots
That are your prisoners—

  Hot.   I'll keep them all.   225
By God, he shall not have a Scot of them!
No, if a Scot would save his soul, he shall not.
I'll keep them, by this hand!

Wor.   You start away
And lend no ear unto my purposes.   230
Those prisoners you shall keep.

  Hot.   Nay, I will! That's flat!
He said he would not ransom Mortimer,
Forbade my tongue to speak of Mortimer,
But I will find him when he lies asleep,   235
And in his ear I'll hollo "Mortimer."
Nay, I'll have a starling shall be taught to speak
Nothing but "Mortimer," and give it him
To keep his anger still in motion.

  Wor. Hear you, cousin, a word.   240

  Hot. All studies here I solemnly defy
Save how to gall and pinch this Bolingbroke;
And that same sword-and-buckler Prince of Wales:
But that I think his father loves him not
And would be glad he met with some mischance,   245
I would have him poisoned with a pot of ale.

  Wor. Farewell, kinsman. I'll talk to you
When you are better tempered to attend.

  North. Why, what a wasp-stung and impatient fool
Art thou to break into this woman's mood,   250
Tying thine ear to no tongue but thine own!

254. **pismires:** ants.

255. **politician:** crafty schemer.

258. **kept:** resided.

265. **candy deal of courtesy:** i.e., deal of saccharine politeness.

269. **cozeners:** cheaters; with a pun; see I. ii. 124.

272. **stay your leisure:** await your pleasure.

277. **divers:** diverse; various.

282. **bosom:** confidence.

Hot. Why, look you, I am whipped and scourged
    with rods,
Nettled, and stung with pismires when I hear
Of this vile politician, Bolingbroke.   255
In Richard's time—what do you call the place?
A plague upon it! it is in Gloucestershire;
'Twas where the madcap duke his uncle kept,
His uncle York—where I first bowed my knee
Unto this king of smiles, this Bolingbroke—   260
'Sblood!—when you and he came back from Ravens-
    purgh—
    North. At Berkeley Castle.
    Hot. You say true.
Why, what a candy deal of courtesy   265
This fawning greyhound then did proffer me!
"Look when his infant fortune came to age,"
And "gentle Harry Percy," and "kind cousin"—
O, the Devil take such cozeners!—God forgive me!
Good uncle, tell your tale, for I have done.   270
    Wor. Nay, if you have not, to it again.
We will stay your leisure.
    Hot.   I have done, i' faith.
    Wor. Then once more to your Scottish prisoners.
Deliver them up without their ransom straight,   275
And make the Douglas' son your only mean
For powers in Scotland, which, for divers reasons
Which I shall send you written, be assured
Will easily be granted. [*To Northumberland*] You,
    my lord,   280
Your son in Scotland being thus employed,
Shall secretly into the bosom creep

286. **bears hard:** deeply resents.

288. **estimation:** mere surmise.

292. **bring it on:** i.e., call forth its expression.

294. **Before the game is afoot thou still letst slip:** that is, you are so impatient that you can never wait till the moment is right to strike. The imagery is from the loosing of dogs after the quarry.

295. **cannot choose but be:** i.e., must be.

299. **aimed:** planned.

301. **head:** army.

302. **bear ourselves as even as we can:** though we behave as well as we can.

305. **pay us home:** pay us once and for all; i.e., put us out of the way.

311. **suddenly:** without delay.

Of that same noble prelate well-beloved,
The Archbishop.
    Hot.   Of York, is it not?   285
    Wor. True; who bears hard
His brother's death at Bristow, the Lord Scroop.
I speak not this in estimation,
As what I think might be, but what I know
Is ruminated, plotted, and set down,   290
And only stays but to behold the face
Of that occasion that shall bring it on.
    Hot. I smell it. Upon my life, it will do well.
    North. Before the game is afoot thou still letst slip.
    Hot. Why, it cannot choose but be a noble plot.   295
And then the power of Scotland and of York
To join with Mortimer, ha?
    Wor.   And so they shall.
    Hot. In faith, it is exceedingly well aimed.
    Wor. And 'tis no little reason bids us speed   300
To save our heads by raising of a head;
For, bear ourselves as even as we can,
The King will always think him in our debt,
And think we think ourselves unsatisfied,
Till he hath found a time to pay us home.   305
And see already how he doth begin
To make us strangers to his looks of love.
    Hot. He does, he does! We'll be revenged on him.
    Wor. Cousin, farewell. No further go in this
Than I by letters shall direct your course.   310
When time is ripe, which will be suddenly,
I'll steal to Glendower and Lord Mortimer,

313. **at once:** simultaneously; all together.

Where you and Douglas, and our powers at once,
As I will fashion it, shall happily meet,
To bear our fortunes in our own strong arms,   315
Which now we hold at much uncertainty.

   North. Farewell, good brother. We shall thrive, I
      trust.

   Hot. Uncle, adieu. O let the hours be short
Till fields and blows and groans applaud our sport!   320
                         Exeunt.

THE HISTORY OF
HENRY
THE FOURTH
[PART 1]

ACT II

II. i. At an inn at Rochester on the road to London, Gadshill confirms his earlier information that a party of rich travelers is staying at the inn and will set forth shortly. He boasts that he need not fear the hangman's noose because his associates are such powerful personages that if worse comes to worst they will intervene to preserve their own reputations.

—————————————————

Ent. **Carrier:** a commercial deliveryman who transported letters and packages.

1. **four by the day:** 4:00 A.M.

2. **Charles' wain:** Charles' wagon, a popular term for the Great Bear.

5. **Cut:** a horse, so called because of its cut tail.

6. **flocks:** pieces of wool; **point:** front; **jade:** nag; a poor specimen of horseflesh; **wrung in the withers:** pinched or chafed in the upper shoulders.

7. **out of all cess:** beyond measure.

8. **dank:** damp.

9. **next:** quickest; **the bots:** intestinal parasites that infect horses.

15. **stung like a tench:** the tench is a fresh-water fish, spotted with red marks which resemble flea bites.

17. **king christen:** Christian king.

ACT II

Scene I. [Rochester. An inn yard.]

Enter a Carrier with a lantern in his hand.

1. Car. Heigh-ho! an it be not four by the day, I'll
be hanged. Charles' wain is over the new chimney,
and yet our horse not packed.—What, ostler!
Ostler. [*Within*] Anon, anon.
1. Car. I prithee, Tom, beat Cut's saddle, put a few   5
flocks in the point. Poor jade is wrung in the withers
out of all cess.

Enter another Carrier.

2. Car. Peas and beans are as dank here as a dog,
and that is the next way to give poor jades the bots.
This house is turned upside down since Robin Ostler   10
died.
1. Car. Poor fellow never joyed since the price of
oats rose. It was the death of him.
2. Car. I think this be the most villainous house in
all London road for fleas. I am stung like a tench.   15
1. Car. Like a tench? By the mass, there is ne'er a
king christen could be better bit than I have been
since the first cock.

24

19. **jordan:** chamberpot.

20. **your . . . your:** i.e., **chimney** and **chamber-lye** in general; **chamber-lye:** urine.

21. **loach:** a fish which was believed to breed fleas.

24. **gammon:** flitch or side; **gammon** literally means leg or thigh and is still used in England for ham; **razes:** roots.

25. **Charing Cross:** the site of Charing Cross is now alongside Trafalgar Square in the heart of London, but at this time it was a village between the City and Westminster.

26. **pannier:** basket.

29-30. **break the pate on thee:** i.e., bloody your head, not break your skull; **very:** true.

31. **faith:** reliability.

39. **Ay, when? canst tell:** a sarcastic refusal; equivalent to some such expression as "not on your life."

43. **Time enough to go to bed with a candle:** almost anytime. The carrier is not committing himself to the inquisitive Gadshill.

45. **They will along:** that is, they will want to travel.

46. **great charge:** much money, or costly belongings.

2. *Car.* Why, they will allow us ne'er a jordan, and then we leak in your chimney, and your chamber-lye 20 breeds fleas like a loach.

1. *Car.* What, ostler! come away and be hanged! come away!

2. *Car.* I have a gammon of bacon and two razes of ginger, to be delivered as far as Charing Cross. 25

1. *Car.* God's body! the turkeys in my pannier are quite starved. What, ostler! A plague on thee! hast thou never an eye in thy head? Canst not hear? An 'twere not as good deed as drink to break the pate on thee, I am a very villain. Come, and be hanged! Hast 30 no faith in thee?

Enter Gadshill.

Gad. Good morrow, carriers. What's o'clock?

1. *Car.* I think it be two o'clock.

Gad. I prithee lend me thy lantern to see my gelding in the stable. 35

1. *Car.* Nay, by God, soft! I know a trick worth two of that, i' faith.

Gad. I pray thee lend me thine.

2. *Car.* Ay, when? canst tell? Lend me thy lantern, quoth he? Marry, I'll see thee hanged first! 40

Gad. Sirrah carrier, what time do you mean to come to London?

2. *Car.* Time enough to go to bed with a candle, I warrant thee. Come, neighbor Mugs, we'll call up the gentlemen. They will along with company, for 45 they have great charge.   *Exeunt* [*Carriers*].

Gad. What, ho! chamberlain!

48. **At hand, quoth pickpurse:** "right here," said the pickpocket; a proverbial expression. Nothing could be closer than a thief with his hand in your pocket.

49. **even:** just; **fair:** exact.

50-1. **thou variest no more from picking of purses than giving direction doth from laboring:** that is, if not a thief yourself, you give orders to them. The staffs of inns were notorious for their collaboration with thieves, often reporting the arrival of wealthy travelers to confederates who then robbed them.

53-4. **holds current:** remains true; **franklin:** property owner below the rank of gentry.

55. **Wild:** weald; forest.

60. **presently:** at once.

61-2. **Saint Nicholas' clerks:** a slang term for thieves. In Shakespeare's time, Saint Nicholas had become the patron saint for robbers, possibly because of the similarity between Nicholas and "Old Nick" (the Devil); or possibly because in the medieval period he was often pictured with three purses in his hand.

69. **Trojans:** good sports. Elizabethan sentiment favored the Trojans over the Greeks in the war over Helen. "Trojan" was often used as an adjective to describe a person of stalwart valor, a "bully boy" or the like, until apparently in slang usage it came also to be used for a good tavern companion.

73. **foot land-rakers:** vagabonds who steal for a living.

74. **long-staff sixpenny strikers:** petty thieves armed only with staves.

74-5. **mad mustachio purple-hued maltworms:** drunkards whose long mustaches have become stained with drink; **nobility and tranquillity:** i.e., persons of high rank who need not worry about their livelihoods.

Enter *Chamberlain.*

Cham. At hand, quoth pickpurse.

Gad. That's even as fair as "at hand, quoth the chamberlain"; for thou variest no more from picking 50 of purses than giving direction doth from laboring: thou layest the plot how.

Cham. Good morrow, Master Gadshill. It holds current that I told you yesternight. There's a franklin in the Wild of Kent hath brought three hundred 55 marks with him in gold. I heard him tell it to one of his company last night at supper—a kind of auditor, one that hath abundance of charge too, God knows what. They are up already and call for eggs and butter. They will away presently. 60

Gad. Sirrah, if they meet not with Saint Nicholas' clerks, I'll give thee this neck.

Cham. No, I'll none of it. I pray thee keep that for the hangman; for I know thou worshipest Saint Nicholas as truly as a man of falsehood may. 65

Gad. What talkest thou to me of the hangman? If I hang, I'll make a fat pair of gallows; for if I hang, old Sir John hangs with me, and thou knowest he is no starveling. Tut! there are other Trojans that thou dreamst not of, the which for sport sake are content 70 to do the profession some grace; that would (if matters should be looked into) for their own credit sake make all whole. I am joined with no foot land-rakers, no long-staff sixpenny strikers, none of these mad mustachio purple-hued maltworms; but with nobility 75

76. **burgomasters:** officials; **great oneyers:** "great one-ers"; i.e., great personages.

77. **hold in:** keep quiet.

78. **speak sooner than drink:** i.e., would rather say the word to halt a traveler than ask for a drink.

82. **boots:** booty; profit.

83. **boots:** an obvious pun.

84. **in foul way:** on wet roads, with a pun.

85. **liquored:** greased, in two senses: bribed and oiled.

86-7. **as in a castle:** that is, as safely as a castle stands a siege; **the receipt of fernseed:** fernseed is so hard to see that it is almost invisible. In Elizabethan folklore, **fernseed** could therefore make the user of it invisible. **Receipt** is equivalent to recipe.

92. **purchase:** spoil; plunder.

95. **Go to; "homo" is a common name to all men:** get along—all men belong to the genus "homo" (man).

97. **muddy:** dull; stupid.

▬▬▬▬▬▬▬▬▬▬▬▬▬▬▬▬▬▬▬▬▬▬

II. ii. Falstaff and his company lie in wait for the wealthy travelers. After Falstaff and the others have tied up the travelers and robbed them, Prince Henry and Poins set upon them in disguise; the four thieves run away; and the Prince and Poins are left in possession of the loot with a good joke on their friends.

▬▬▬▬▬▬▬▬▬▬▬▬▬▬▬▬▬

2. **frets like a gummed velvet:** a proverbial metaphor. Velvet and taffeta were sometimes stiffened with gum, with the result that the fabric "fretted" (wore) more readily.

and tranquillity, burgomasters and great oneyers, such
as can hold in, such as will strike sooner than speak,
and speak sooner than drink, and drink sooner than
pray; and yet, zounds, I lie; for they pray continually
to their saint, the commonwealth, or rather, not pray   80
to her, but prey on her, for they ride up and down on
her and make her their boots.

Cham. What, the commonwealth their boots? Will
she hold out water in foul way?

Gad. She will, she will! Justice hath liquored her.   85
We steal as in a castle, cocksure. We have the receipt
of fernseed, we walk invisible.

Cham. Nay, by my faith, I think you are more be-
holding to the night than to fernseed for your walking
invisible.   90

Gad. Give me thy hand. Thou shalt have a share in
our purchase, as I am a true man.

Cham. Nay, rather let me have it, as you are a
false thief.

Gad. Go to; "homo" is a common name to all men.   95
Bid the ostler bring my gelding out of the stable.
Farewell, you muddy knave.

[*Exeunt.*]

Scene II. [The highway near Gad's Hill.]

Enter *Prince, Poins, Peto,* and [*Bardolph*].

Poins. Come, shelter, shelter! I have removed Falstaff's horse, and he frets like a gummed velvet.

3. **close:** concealed.

13. **squire:** square or rule.

18. **medicines:** love potions.

24. **veriest:** most absolute; see II. i. 30; **varlet:** rascal.

Carrier's horse with panniers.
From Hugh Alley, *A Caveat for the City of London* (1598).

Prince. Stand close. [*They hide.*]

Enter *Falstaff*.

Fal. Poins! Poins, and be hanged! Poins!

Prince. [*Comes forward*] Peace, ye fat-kidneyed 5
rascal! What a brawling dost thou keep!

Fal. Where's Poins, Hal?

Prince. He is walked up to the top of the hill; I'll
go seek him. [*Hides.*]

Fal. I am accursed to rob in that thief's company. 10
The rascal hath removed my horse and tied him I
know not where. If I travel but four foot by the
squire further afoot, I shall break my wind. Well, I
doubt not but to die a fair death for all this, if I
'scape hanging for killing that rogue. I have forsworn 15
his company hourly any time this two-and-twenty
years, and yet I am bewitched with the rogue's company. If the rascal have not given me medicines to
make me love him, I'll be hanged. It could not be
else: I have drunk medicines. Poins! Hal! A plague 20
upon you both! Bardolph! Peto! I'll starve ere I'll rob
a foot further. An 'twere not as good a deed as drink
to turn true man and to leave these rogues, I am the
veriest varlet that ever chewed with a tooth. Eight
yards of uneven ground is threescore and ten miles 25
afoot with me, and the stony-hearted villains know it
well enough. A plague upon it when thieves cannot
be true one to another! (*They whistle.*) Whew! A
plague upon you all! Give me my horse, you rogues!
give me my horse and be hanged! 30

37. **colt:** fool.

43-4. **heir-apparent garters:** to "hang oneself in one's own garters" was a proverbial expression. Falstaff refers to the Prince's possession of the Order of the Garter as heir to the throne; **peach:** turn informer.

46-7. **is so forward:** goes so far.

53. **Case ye:** i.e., **"On with your vizards!"**

Prince. [*Steps forward*] Peace, ye fat-guts! Lie
down, lay thine ear close to the ground, and list if
thou canst hear the tread of travelers.

Fal. Have you any levers to lift me up again, being down? 'Sblood, I'll not bear mine own flesh so   35
far afoot again for all the coin in thy father's exchequer. What a plague mean ye to colt me thus?

Prince. Thou liest; thou art not colted, thou art
uncolted.

Fal. I prithee, good Prince Hal, help me to my   40
horse, good king's son.

Prince. Out, ye rogue! Shall I be your ostler?

Fal. Go hang thyself in thine own heir-apparent
garters! If I be ta'en, I'll peach for this. An I have not
ballads made on you all, and sung to filthy tunes, let   45
a cup of sack be my poison. When a jest is so forward—and afoot too—I hate it.

Enter *Gadshill*.

Gad. Stand!

Fal. So I do, against my will.

Poins. [*Steps forward*] O, 'tis our setter; I know his   50
voice.

Bar. What news?

Gad. Case ye, case ye! On with your vizards!
There's money of the King's coming down the hill;
'tis going to the King's exchequer.   55

Fal. You lie, ye rogue! 'Tis going to the King's
tavern.

Gad. There's enough to make us all.

60. **front:** confront.

76. **hard:** near.

77. **happy man be his dole:** may we have good luck.

Fal. To be hanged.

Prince. Sirs, you four shall front them in the nar-　60
row lane; Ned Poins and I will walk lower. If they
'scape from your encounter, then they light on us.

Peto. How many be there of them?

Gad. Some eight or ten.

Fal. Zounds, will they not rob us?　65

Prince. What, a coward, Sir John Paunch?

Fal. Indeed, I am not John of Gaunt, your grandfather, but yet no coward, Hal.

Prince. Well, we leave that to the proof.

Poins. Sirrah Jack, thy horse stands behind the　70
hedge. When thou needst him, there thou shalt find
him. Farewell and stand fast.

Fal. Now cannot I strike him, if I should be hanged.

Prince [*Aside to Poins*] Ned, where are our dis-
guises?　75

Poins. [*Aside to Prince*] Here, hard by. Stand close.

　　　　　　　　　　[*Exeunt Prince and Poins.*]

Fal. Now, my masters, happy man be his dole,
say I. Every man to his business.

Enter the *Travelers*.

Trav. Come, neighbor. The boy shall lead our
horses down the hill; we'll walk afoot awhile and　80
ease our legs.

Thieves. Stand!

Trav. Jesus bless us!

Fal. Strike! down with them! cut the villains'

85. **whoreson:** a term of jocular abuse; **caterpillars:** parasites.

88. **gorbellied:** great-bellied; fat.

89. **chuffs:** misers; **store:** total sum of wealth.

91. **grand jurors:** men of substance, such as were chosen to serve as grand jurors.

94. **argument:** subject matter.

99. **arrant:** downright; absolute; **there's no equity stirring:** sound judgment is nonexistent.

throats! Ah, whoreson caterpillars! bacon-fed knaves!   85
they hate us youth. Down with them! fleece them!

Trav. O, we are undone, both we and ours forever!

Fal. Hang ye, gorbellied knaves, are ye undone?
No, ye fat chuffs; I would your store were here! On,
bacons, on! What, ye knaves! young men must live.   90
You are grand jurors, are ye? We'll jure ye, faith!

> *Here they rob them and bind them. Exeunt.*

Enter the *Prince* and *Poins* [in buckram suits].

Prince. The thieves have bound the true men. Now
could thou and I rob the thieves and go merrily to
London, it would be argument for a week, laughter
for a month, and a good jest forever.   95

Poins. Stand close! I hear them coming.

> [*They stand aside.*]

Enter the *Thieves* again.

Fal. Come, my masters, let us share, and then to
horse before day. An the Prince and Poins be not
two arrant cowards, there's no equity stirring. There's
no more valor in that Poins than in a wild duck.   100

Prince. Your money!

Poins. Villains!

*As they are sharing, the Prince and Poins set upon
them. They all run away, and Falstaff, after a blow or
two, runs away too, leaving the booty behind them.*

Prince. Got with much ease. Now merrily to horse.
The thieves are all scattered, and possessed with fear

107. **lards the lean earth:** sweat was believed to be actual drops of fat melted when the body became overheated. Thus, Falstaff is pictured as enriching the earth with his sweat.

110. **How the fat rogue roared:** "fat" is included from the Quarto fragment in the Folger and is not to be found in other texts. This fragment may represent the sole survival of a quarto antedating the First Quarto of 1598.

⸻

II. iii. Hotspur is irritated by a letter from one who will not join his league because the outcome is too uncertain. His wife has observed that something serious is on his mind and seeks his confidence, but he will reveal nothing more than the fact that he must be off on his horse at once. He promises that she will follow him the next day.

⸻

Ent. **solus:** alone.

2. **well contented:** pleased enough; **in respect:** because.

9-10. **out of this nettle, danger, we pluck this flower, safety:** Shakespeare's use of an Elizabethan proverb: "Danger and delight grow both upon one stalk."

12. **unsorted:** unsuitable; not chosen with proper care.

13. **for the counterpoise of:** to offset.

15. **hind:** countryman; hayseed.

18-9. **full of expectation:** promising well.

so strongly that they dare not meet each other: each   105
takes his fellow for an officer. Away, good Ned. Falstaff sweats to death and lards the lean earth as he
walks along. Were't not for laughing, I should pity
him.

Poins. How the fat rogue roared!   110

           Exeunt.

Scene III. [Warkworth Castle.]

Enter Hotspur solus, reading a letter.

Hot. "But, for mine own part, my lord, I could be
well contented to be there, in respect of the love I
bear your house." He could be contented—why is he
not then? In respect of the love he bears our house!
He shows in this he loves his own barn better than   5
he loves our house. Let me see some more. "The purpose you undertake is dangerous"—why, that's certain! 'Tis dangerous to take a cold, to sleep, to drink;
but I tell you, my lord fool, out of this nettle, danger,
we pluck this flower, safety. "The purpose you under-   10
take is dangerous, the friends you have named uncertain, the time itself unsorted, and your whole
plot too light for the counterpoise of so great an opposition." Say you so, say you so? I say unto you
again, you are a shallow, cowardly hind, and you   15
lie. What a lack-brain is this! By the Lord, our plot
is a good plot as ever was laid; our friends true and
constant: a good plot, good friends, and full of ex-

29. **pagan:** i.e., an unbeliever; lacking in faith.

32. **divide myself and go to buffets:** divide myself into two parts so that one part could beat the other.

42. **stomach:** appetite.

pectation; an excellent plot, very good friends. What
a frosty-spirited rogue is this! Why, my Lord of York   20
commends the plot and the general course of the
action. Zounds, an I were now by this rascal, I could
brain him with his lady's fan. Is there not my father,
my uncle, and myself; Lord Edmund Mortimer, my
Lord of York, and Owen Glendower? Is there not,   25
besides, the Douglas? Have I not all their letters to
meet me in arms by the ninth of the next month, and
are they not some of them set forward already? What
a pagan rascal is this! an infidel! Ha! you shall see
now, in very sincerity of fear and cold heart will he   30
to the King and lay open all our proceedings. O, I
could divide myself and go to buffets for moving
such a dish of skim milk with so honorable an action!
Hang him, let him tell the King! we are prepared. I
will set forward tonight.   35

Enter his Lady.

How now, Kate? I must leave you within these two
    hours.
    Lady. O my good lord, why are you thus alone?
For what offense have I this fortnight been
A banished woman from my Harry's bed?   40
Tell me, sweet lord, what is't that takes from thee
Thy stomach, pleasure, and thy golden sleep?
Why dost thou bend thine eyes upon the earth,
And start so often when thou sitst alone?
Why hast thou lost the fresh blood in thy cheeks   45
And given my treasures and my rights of thee

48. **faint:** fretful.

50. **manage:** horsemanship, from the French *manège*.

53. **palisadoes:** barricades of stakes; **frontiers:** the outermost fortifications.

54. **basilisks . . . culverin:** types of cannon.

56. **heady:** headlong.

61. **motions:** that is, signs of emotion.

62-3. **restrain their breath/On some great sudden hest:** that is, steel themselves to answer a great demand on their resources. **Hest** means command; **portents:** omens.

65. **heavy:** grave and perilous; see I. i. 37.

72. **even:** just; see II. i. 49.

To thick-eyed musing and cursed melancholy?
In thy faint slumbers I by thee have watched,
And heard thee murmur tales of iron wars,
Speak terms of manage to thy bounding steed,   50
Cry "Courage! to the field!" And thou hast talked
Of sallies and retires, of trenches, tents,
Of palisadoes, frontiers, parapets,
Of basilisks, of cannon, culverin,
Of prisoners' ransom, and of soldiers slain,   55
And all the currents of a heady fight.
Thy spirit within thee hath been so at war,
And thus hath so bestirred thee in thy sleep,
That beads of sweat have stood upon thy brow
Like bubbles in a late-disturbed stream,   60
And in thy face strange motions have appeared,
Such as we see when men restrain their breath
On some great sudden hest. O what portents are
    these?
Some heavy business hath my lord in hand,   65
And I must know it, else he loves me not.
    Hot. What, ho!

[Enter a *Servant*.]

            Is Gilliams with the packet gone?
    Ser. He is, my lord, an hour ago.
    Hot. Hath Butler brought those horses from the   70
    sheriff?
    Ser. One horse, my lord, he brought even now.
    Hot. What horse? A roan, a crop-ear, is it not?
    Ser. It is, my lord.

76. **back him straight:** be on his back instantly; **espérance:** the Percy motto and battle cry was *"Espérance en Dieu"* (Hope in God).

83. **A weasel hath not such a deal of spleen:** The Elizabethans attributed a nervous and irritable temperament to the weasel, and the spleen was considered the source of anger and irritation.

88. **line:** reinforce; back.

97. **mammets:** dolls.

99. **pass them current: a cracked crown** (gold coin) was not negotiable, but Hotspur jokes that such is the current state of affairs that **cracked crowns** (broken heads) must be accepted; **Gods me:** God save me.

Hot.   That roan shall be my throne.   75
Well, I will back him straight. O espérance!
Bid Butler lead him forth into the park.

                         [*Exit Servant.*]

   Lady. But hear you, my lord.
   Hot. What sayst thou, my lady?
   Lady. What is it carries you away?   80
   Hot. Why, my horse, my love—my horse!
   Lady. Out, you mad-headed ape!
A weasel hath not such a deal of spleen
As you are tossed with. In faith,
I'll know your business, Harry; that I will!   85
I fear my brother Mortimer doth stir
About his title and hath sent for you
To line his enterprise; but if you go—
   Hot. So far afoot, I shall be weary, love.
   Lady. Come, come, you paraquito, answer me   90
Directly unto this question that I ask.
In faith, I'll break thy little finger, Harry,
An if thou wilt not tell me all things true.
   Hot. Away, away, you trifler! Love? I love thee
     not;   95
I care not for thee, Kate. This is no world
To play with mammets and to tilt with lips.
We must have bloody noses and cracked crowns,
And pass them current too. Gods me, my horse!
What sayst thou, Kate? What wouldst thou have   100
     with me?
   Lady. Do you not love me? do you not indeed?
Well, do not then; for since you love me not,
I will not love myself. Do you not love me?

110. **reason whereabout:** discuss why I am going.

124. **of force:** of necessity.

━━━━━━━━━━━━━━━━━━━━━━━━━━━━━

II. iv. Prince Hal, in high spirits at the success of the prank he and Poins have played on Falstaff, exercises his wit at the expense of an apprentice tapster at the Boar's Head Tavern. Falstaff and his fellow rogues come in and the fat knight accuses the Prince and Poins of cowardice because (so he thinks) they fled before the robbery was brought off. As expected, he has a dramatic story of defending himself against a whole band of armed men. The Prince finally reveals the deception and accuses Falstaff, in turn, of cowardice. Falstaff, however, refuses to be put down, and claims that he recognized his assailants but could not harm the "true Prince." He and the Prince improvise an imaginary interview between the King and his heir, which reveals Falstaff's concern that the Prince will one day abandon him. The game is interrupted by a visit from the sheriff seeking the men who robbed the travelers. Falstaff retires behind an arras where he falls asleep, while the Prince deals with the law. As the scene concludes, Hal reveals that they must be off to war in a short time; Falstaff will have an infantry company and Peto will also have an honorable post.

━━━━━━━━━━━━━━━━━━━━━

1. **fat-room:** vat-room, that is, taproom.

Nay, tell me if you speak in jest or no.   105
   Hot. Come, wilt thou see me ride?
And when I am a-horseback, I will swear
I love thee infinitely. But hark you, Kate:
I must not have you henceforth question me
Whither I go, nor reason whereabout.   110
Whither I must, I must, and to conclude,
This evening must I leave you, gentle Kate.
I know you wise, but yet no farther wise
Than Harry Percy's wife; constant you are,
But yet a woman; and for secrecy,   115
No lady closer, for I well believe
Thou wilt not utter what thou dost not know,
And so far will I trust thee, gentle Kate.
   Lady. How? so far?
   Hot. Not an inch further. But hark you, Kate: 120
Whither I go, thither shall you go too;
Today will I set forth, tomorrow you.
Will this content you, Kate?
   Lady.   It must of force.

                                   Exeunt.

Scene IV. [London. The Boar's Head Tavern in
Eastcheap.]

Enter *Prince* and *Poins.*

   Prince. Ned, prithee come out of that fat-room and
lend me thy hand to laugh a little.
   Poins. Where hast been, Hal?

4. **loggerheads:** blockheads.

6. **bass-string:** i.e., lowest note.

7. **a leash:** three in number. Three dogs usually composed **a leash; drawers:** tapsters.

9. **Take it . . . upon:** swear by.

11. **proud Jack:** presumptuous fellow. **Jack** was also a term for a drinking vessel.

12. **Corinthian:** sport; one who enjoys a life of pleasure; **lad of mettle:** fellow of spirit.

15-6. **dyeing scarlet:** the urine of heavy drinkers was used for certain scarlet dyes; **watering:** drinking.

17. **play it off:** drink it down.

23. **pennyworth of sugar:** small packets of sugar were kept on hand for customers who wished to sweeten their sack.

24. **under-skinker:** tapster's apprentice. "Skink" means "pour" from the German *schenken.*

27-8. **Anon:** coming at once. The reply to a customer's call for service; **Score a pint of bastard in the Half-moon:** i.e., charge the customers in the Half-moon (the name of a room in the tavern) with a pint of sweet wine. **Bastard** was the name of a variety of Spanish wine.

30. **puny:** i.e., because he is only an assistant drawer; raw.

34. **precedent:** an example to follow; that is, a joke worth remembering.

Prince. With three or four loggerheads amongst
three or fourscore hogsheads. I have sounded the   5
very bass-string of humility. Sirrah, I am sworn brother to a leash of drawers and can call them all by
their christen names, as Tom, Dick, and Francis.
They take it already upon their salvation that, though
I be but Prince of Wales, yet I am the king of cour-   10
tesy, and tell me flatly I am no proud Jack like Falstaff, but a Corinthian, a lad of mettle, a good boy
(by the Lord, so they call me!), and when I am
King of England I shall command all the good lads
in Eastcheap. They call drinking deep, dyeing scar-   15
let; and when you breathe in your watering, they
cry "hem!" and bid you play it off. To conclude, I
am so good a proficient in one quarter of an hour
that I can drink with any tinker in his own language
during my life. I tell thee, Ned, thou hast lost much   20
honor that thou wert not with me in this action. But,
sweet Ned—to sweeten which name of Ned, I give
thee this pennyworth of sugar, clapped even now into
my hand by an under-skinker, one that never spake
other English in his life than "Eight shillings and   25
sixpence," and "You are welcome," with this shrill
addition, "Anon, anon, sir! Score a pint of bastard
in the Half-moon," or so—but, Ned, to drive away
the time till Falstaff come, I prithee do thou stand
in some by-room while I question my puny drawer   30
to what end he gave me the sugar; and do thou never
leave calling "Francis!" that his tale to me may be
nothing but "Anon!" Step aside, and I'll show thee
a precedent.

38-9. Pomgarnet: Pomegranate, the name of another room in the tavern.

42. serve: serve his apprenticeship.

Driving cattle to Eastcheap Market.
From Hugh Alley, *A Caveat for the City of London* (1598).

Poins. Francis!   35
Prince. Thou art perfect.
Poins. Francis!   [*Exit Poins.*]

Enter [*Francis,* a] Drawer.

Fran. Anon, anon, sir.—Look down into the Pom-
garnet, Ralph.
Prince. Come hither, Francis.   40
Fran. My lord?
Prince. How long hast thou to serve, Francis?
Fran. Forsooth, five years, and as much as to—
Poins. [*Within*] Francis!
Fran. Anon, anon, sir.   45
Prince. Five year! by'r Lady, a long lease for the
clinking of pewter. But, Francis, darest thou be so
valiant as to play the coward with thy indenture and
show it a fair pair of heels and run from it?
Fran. O Lord, sir, I'll be sworn upon all the books   50
in England I could find in my heart—
Poins. [*Within*] Francis!
Fran. Anon, sir.
Prince. How old art thou, Francis?
Fran. Let me see: about Michaelmas next I shall   55
be—
Poins. [*Within*] Francis!
Fran. Anon, sir. Pray stay a little, my lord.
Prince. Nay, but hark you, Francis. For the sugar
thou gavest me—'twas a pennyworth, was't not?   60
Fran. O Lord! I would it had been two!

71-2. not-pated: short-haired; **agate-ring:** wearing an agate-stone ring; **puke-stocking:** dark woolen-stockinged; **caddis-garter:** gartered with caddis, a kind of tape; **Spanish-pouch:** a purse suspended from the waist, from which mine host presumably made change.

74-7. Why . . . much: the Prince is engaged in a bit of foolery with the slow-witted waiter, Francis, and confuses him (as well as the reader) with a few lines of bombast that have little meaning; **sully:** stain.

S.D. after l. 81. amazed: completely bewildered; dumbstruck.

Prince. I will give thee for it a thousand pound.
Ask me when thou wilt, and thou shalt have it.

Poins. [*Within*] Francis!

Fran. Anon, anon.   65

Prince. Anon, Francis? No, Francis; but tomorrow, Francis; or, Francis, a Thursday; or indeed,
Francis, when thou wilt. But, Francis—

Fran. My lord?

Prince. Wilt thou rob this leathern-jerkin, crystal-   70
button, not-pated, agate-ring, puke-stocking, caddis-garter, smooth-tongue, Spanish-pouch—

Fran. O Lord, sir, who do you mean?

Prince. Why then, your brown bastard is your only
drink; for look you, Francis, your white canvas doub-   75
let will sully. In Barbary, sir, it cannot come to so
much.

Fran. What, sir?

Poins. [*Within*] Francis!

Prince. Away, you rogue! Dost thou not hear them   80
call?

> *Here they both call him. The Drawer stands*
> *amazed, not knowing which way to go.*

Enter *Vintner.*

Vint. What, standst thou still, and hearest such a
calling? Look to the guests within. [*Exit Francis.*]
My lord, old Sir John, with half a dozen more, are
at the door. Shall I let them in?   85

Prince. Let them alone awhile, and then open the
door. [*Exit Vintner.*] Poins!

92. **what cunning match have you made:** i.e., what was the point of teasing the waiter in this fashion?

94. **of all humors:** that is, in a fanciful mood, ready to indulge every whim that occurs to me.

96. **pupil age:** youth.

103. **parcel:** part; i.e., one item.

104. **kills me:** the ethical dative grammatical construction, meaning simply "kills."

109. **drench:** restorative dose.

A tavern waiter.
From a seventeenth-century ballad.

Poins. [*Within*] Anon, anon, sir.

Enter *Poins*.

Prince. Sirrah, Falstaff and the rest of the thieves
are at the door. Shall we be merry?   90
Poins. As merry as crickets, my lad. But hark ye;
what cunning match have you made with this jest
of the drawer? Come, what's the issue?
Prince. I am now of all humors that have showed
themselves humors since the old days of goodman 95
Adam to the pupil age of this present twelve o'clock
at midnight.

[Re-enter *Francis*.]

What's o'clock, Francis?
Fran. Anon, anon, sir.   [*Exit.*]
Prince. That ever this fellow should have fewer 100
words than a parrot, and yet the son of a woman!
His industry is upstairs and downstairs, his eloquence
the parcel of a reckoning. I am not yet of Percy's
mind, the Hotspur of the North; he that kills me
some six or seven dozen of Scots at a breakfast, 105
washes his hands, and says to his wife, "Fie upon
this quiet life! I want work." "O my sweet Harry,"
says she, "how many hast thou killed today?" "Give
my roan horse a drench," says he, and answers "Some
fourteen," an hour after, "a trifle, a trifle." I prithee 110
call in Falstaff. I'll play Percy, and that damned

112. **brawn:** fat porker; **"Rivo!":** a popular exclamation to accompany a deep draught. The meaning is akin to "down the hatch," "bottoms up," or "cheers."

117. **netherstocks:** stockings. Breeches were known as "upper stocks."

120. **virtue:** manliness; valor.

121. **Titan:** i.e., the sun.

124. **compound:** i.e., melting butter.

125. **lime in this sack:** wine was adulterated with lime to make it both dryer and brighter.

130-31. **shotten herring:** a herring that has spawned; i.e., thin.

133. **the while:** these times.

133-34. **a weaver:** famous as a class for their love of singing and, since many belonged to Puritanical sects, of psalm-singing in particular.

brawn shall play Dame Mortimer his wife. "Rivo!"
says the drunkard. Call in ribs, call in tallow.

Enter *Falstaff,* [*Gadshill, Bardolph,* and *Peto,*
followed by *Francis* with wine].

Poins. Welcome, Jack. Where hast thou been?
Fal. A plague of all cowards, I say, and a venge- 115
ance too! Marry and amen! Give me a cup of sack,
boy. Ere I lead this life long, I'll sew netherstocks,
and mend them and foot them too. A plague of all
cowards! Give me a cup of sack, rogue. Is there no
virtue extant?   *He drinketh.* 120
Prince. Didst thou never see Titan kiss a dish of
butter (pitiful-hearted Titan!) that melted at the
sweet tale of the sun's? If thou didst, then behold that
compound.
Fal. You rogue, here's lime in this sack too! There 125
is nothing but roguery to be found in villainous man.
Yet a coward is worse than a cup of sack with lime
in it—a villainous coward! Go thy ways, old Jack, die
when thou wilt; if manhood, good manhood, be not
forgot upon the face of the earth, then am I a shotten 130
herring. There lives not three good men unhanged in
England; and one of them is fat, and grows old. God
help the while! A bad world, I say. I would I were a
weaver; I could sing psalms or anything. A plague
of all cowards, I say still!   135
Prince. How now, woolsack? What mutter you?
Fal. A king's son! If I do not beat thee out of thy
kingdom with a dagger of lath and drive all thy sub-

157. **All is one for that:** that doesn't matter.

166. **at half-sword with:** half a sword's length from; engaged in close fighting with.

169. **hose:** breeches and stockings together were commonly called **hose;** Falstaff undoubtedly means breeches here.

Drinking in a tavern.
From a seventeenth-century ballad.

jects afore thee like a flock of wild geese, I'll never
wear hair on my face more. You Prince of Wales?   140

Prince. Why, you whoreson round man, what's the
matter?

Fal. Are not you a coward? Answer me to that—
and Poins there?

Poins. Zounds, ye fat paunch, an ye call me coward, 145
by the Lord, I'll stab thee.

Fal. I call thee coward? I'll see thee damned ere
I call thee coward, but I would give a thousand
pound I could run as fast as thou canst. You are
straight enough in the shoulders; you care not 150
who sees your back. Call you that backing of your
friends? A plague upon such backing! Give me them
that will face me. Give me a cup of sack. I am a
rogue if I drunk today.

Prince. O villain! thy lips are scarce wiped since 155
thou drunkst last.

Fal. All is one for that. (*He drinketh.*) A plague
of all cowards, still say I.

Prince. What's the matter?

Fal. What's the matter? There be four of us here 160
have ta'en a thousand pound this day morning.

Prince. Where is it, Jack? where is it?

Fal. Where is it? Taken from us it is. A hundred
upon poor four of us!

Prince. What, a hundred, man?   165

Fal. I am a rogue if I were not at half-sword with
a dozen of them two hours together. I have 'scaped
by miracle. I am eight times thrust through the
doublet, four through the hose; my buckler cut

171. ecce signum: behold this evidence; **dealt:** i.e., fought.

193. peppered: finished; given death blows to.

194. paid: given their quietus; killed; see I. iii. 305.

196. horse: an animal held in contempt.

197. ward: posture of defense; see I. ii. 193.

Fighting with sword and buckler.
From Camillo Agrippa, *Trattato di scientia d'arme* (1568).

through and through; my sword hacked like a hand- 170
saw—ecce signum! I never dealt better since I was
a man. All would not do. A plague of all cowards!
Let them speak. If they speak more or less than truth,
they are villains and the sons of darkness.

Prince. Speak, sirs. How was it?   175

Gad. We four set upon some dozen—

Fal. Sixteen at least, my lord.

Gad. And bound them.

Peto. No, no, they were not bound.

Fal. You rogue, they were bound, every man of 180
them, or I am a Jew else—an Ebrew Jew.

Gad. As we were sharing, some six or seven fresh
men set upon us—

Fal. And unbound the rest, and then come in the
other.   185

Prince. What, fought you with them all?

Fal. All? I know not what you call all, but if I
fought not with fifty of them, I am a bunch of radish!
If there were not two or three and fifty upon poor
old Jack, then am I no two-legged creature.   190

Prince. Pray God you have not murd'red some of
them.

Fal. Nay, that's past praying for. I have peppered
two of them. Two I am sure I have paid, two rogues
in buckram suits. I tell thee what, Hal—if I tell thee 195
a lie, spit in my face, call me horse. Thou knowest
my old ward. Here I lay, and thus I bore my point.
Four rogues in buckram let drive at me.

Prince. What, four? Thou saidst but two even now.

Fal. Four, Hal. I told thee four.   200

202. **afront:** abreast; **mainly:** violently; vigorously.

204. **target:** buckler; shield.

209. **these hilts:** the sword hilt, being divided by the handle and the blade, was often spoken of in the plural. It was common to swear on the cross thus formed.

213. **mark:** the Prince warns that he not only hears Falstaff, he is also "on to" him.

217. **points:** Falstaff means sword points, but Poins replies as though he meant the lacings which held the breeches, stockings, and doublet together.

220. **a thought:** the speed of thought.

225. **Kendal green:** a cloth made in Kendal, Westmoreland; also associated with Robin Hood and his men.

229. **gross:** huge.

230. **knotty-pated:** blockheaded.

231. **tallow-catch:** ball of tallow.

Poins. Ay, ay, he said four.

Fal. These four came all afront and mainly thrust at me. I made me no more ado but took all their seven points in my target, thus.

Prince. Seven? Why, there were but four even 205 now.

Fal. In buckram?

Poins. Ay, four, in buckram suits.

Fal. Seven, by these hilts, or I am a villain else.

Prince. [*Aside to Poins*] Prithee let him alone. We 210 shall have more anon.

Fal. Dost thou hear me, Hal?

Prince. Ay, and mark thee too, Jack.

Fal. Do so, for it is worth the list'ning to. These nine in buckram that I told thee of— 215

Prince. So, two more already.

Fal. Their points being broken—

Poins. Down fell their hose.

Fal. Began to give me ground; but I followed me close, came in, foot and hand, and with a thought 220 seven of the eleven I paid.

Prince. O monstrous! Eleven buckram men grown out of two!

Fal. But, as the Devil would have it, three misbegotten knaves in Kendal green came at my back and 225 let drive at me; for it was so dark, Hal, that thou couldst not see thy hand.

Prince. These lies are like their father that begets them—gross as a mountain, open, palpable. Why, thou clay-brained guts, thou knotty-pated fool, thou 230 whoreson obscene greasy tallow-catch—

240. **strappado:** a method of torture which dislocated the joints.

242. **reasons:** a pun made possible by the fact that the word was pronounced "raisins."

245-46. **sanguine:** a man of **sanguine** "humor" (temperament) was supposed to be courageous, optimistic, and amorous. Falstaff shows the last two characteristics, but not the first.

249. **neat's:** cow's; **stockfish:** dried cod.

251. **tuck:** rapier.

Fal. What, art thou mad? art thou mad? Is not the truth the truth?

Prince. Why, how couldst thou know these men in Kendal green when it was so dark thou couldst not 235 see thy hand? Come, tell us your reason. What sayest thou to this?

Poins. Come, your reason, Jack, your reason.

Fal. What, upon compulsion? Zounds, an I were at the strappado or all the racks in the world, I 240 would not tell you on compulsion. Give you a reason on compulsion? If reasons were as plentiful as black-berries, I would give no man a reason upon com-pulsion, I.

Prince. I'll be no longer guilty of this sin; this san- 245 guine coward, this bed-presser, this horseback-breaker, this huge hill of flesh—

Fal. 'Sblood, you starveling, you eel-skin, you dried neat's-tongue, you bull's pizzle, you stockfish—O for breath to utter what is like thee!—you tailor's yard, 250 you sheath, you bowcase, you vile standing tuck!

Prince. Well, breathe awhile, and then to it again; and when thou hast tired thyself in base comparisons, hear me speak but this.

Poins. Mark, Jack.   255

Prince. We two saw you four set on four, and bound them and were masters of their wealth. Mark now how a plain tale shall put you down. Then did we two set on you four and, with a word, outfaced you from your prize, and have it; yea, and can show 260 it you here in the house. And, Falstaff, you carried your guts away as nimbly, with as quick dexterity,

266. starting hole: hiding place; cover-up.

281. Watch: remain wakeful and have a merry time. Falstaff quotes Matthew 26:41: "Watch and pray, that ye enter not into temptation."

285. argument: subject matter; see II. ii. 94.

Characteristic Englishwoman of the type of Mistress Quickly.
From a seventeenth-century ballad.

and roared for mercy, and still run and roared, as
ever I heard bullcalf. What a slave art thou to hack
thy sword as thou hast done, and then say it was in   265
fight! What trick, what device, what starting hole
canst thou now find out to hide thee from this open
and apparent shame?

Poins. Come, let's hear, Jack. What trick hast thou
now?   270

Fal. By the Lord, I knew ye as well as he that
made ye. Why, hear you, my masters. Was it for me
to kill the heir apparent? Should I turn upon the true
prince? Why, thou knowest I am as valiant as Her-
cules, but beware instinct. The lion will not touch the   275
true prince. Instinct is a great matter. I was now a
coward on instinct. I shall think the better of myself,
and thee, during my life—I for a valiant lion, and
thou for a true prince. But, by the Lord, lads, I am
glad you have the money. Hostess, clap to the doors.   280
Watch tonight, pray tomorrow. Gallants, lads, boys,
hearts of gold, all the titles of good fellowship come
to you! What, shall we be merry? Shall we have a
play extempore?

Prince. Content—and the argument shall be thy   285
running away.

Fal. Ah, no more of that, Hal, an thou lovest me!

Enter *Hostess*.

Hos. O Jesu, my lord the Prince!

Prince. How now, my lady the hostess? What sayst
thou to me?   290

294-5. **a royal man:** see I. ii. 143 for a similar pun. A **noble** was a coin worth six shillings and eightpence; while a **royal** was worth ten shillings.

298. **gravity:** the old man.

319. **with the manner:** in the act; with the goods.

320. **blushed extempore:** i.e., had a permanently red face.

Hos. Marry, my lord, there is a noble man of the court at door would speak with you. He says he comes from your father.

Prince. Give him as much as will make him a royal man, and send him back again to my mother.   295

Fal. What manner of man is he?

Hos. An old man.

Fal. What doth gravity out of his bed at midnight? Shall I give him his answer?

Prince. Prithee do, Jack.   300

Fal. Faith, and I'll send him packing.   *Exit.*

Prince. Now, sirs. By'r Lady, you fought fair; so did you, Peto; so did you, Bardolph. You are lions too, you ran away upon instinct, you will not touch the true prince; no—fie!   305

Bar. Faith, I ran when I saw others run.

Prince. Tell me now in earnest, how came Falstaff's sword so hacked?

Peto. Why, he hacked it with his dagger, and said he would swear truth out of England but he would 310 make you believe it was done in fight, and persuaded us to do the like.

Bar. Yea, and to tickle our noses with speargrass to make them bleed, and then to beslubber our garments with it and swear it was the blood of true men. 315 I did that I did not this seven year before—I blushed to hear his monstrous devices.

Prince. O villain! thou stolest a cup of sack eighteen years ago and wert taken with the manner, and ever since thou hast blushed extempore. Thou 320

323. **meteors:** a reference to the fiery red splotches on his own face.

324. **exhalations:** i.e., meteors; see I. i. 10-1.

327. **Hot livers and cold purses:** i.e., heavy indulgence in liquor, which has heated his liver and emptied his purse.

328. **Choler:** bile, which also meant a hasty temper; **rightly taken:** correctly understood. The Prince replies that if he were **rightly taken** (appropriately caught) the result would be the hangman's noose.

331. **bombast:** cotton stuffing, used to pad garments. The word also meant high-flown language; the Prince may intend both meanings.

334. **talent:** talon.

340-41. **Amamon:** a fiend; **the bastinado:** a beating; **made Lucifer cuckold:** gave Lucifer his horns. Horns were the symbol of a **cuckold** (a husband whose wife was unfaithful).

342-43. **Welsh hook:** a weapon like a pike.

hadst fire and sword on thy side, and yet thou ranst
away. What instinct hadst thou for it?

Bar. My lord, do you see these meteors? Do you
behold these exhalations?

Prince. I do.   325

Bar. What think you they portend?

Prince. Hot livers and cold purses.

Bar. Choler, my lord, if rightly taken.

Prince. No, if rightly taken, halter.

[Re-]enter *Falstaff.*

Here comes lean Jack; here comes bare-bone. How   330
now, my sweet creature of bombast? How long is't
ago, Jack, since thou sawest thine own knee?

Fal. My own knee? When I was about thy years,
Hal, I was not an eagle's talent in the waist; I could
have crept into any alderman's thumb-ring. A plague   335
of sighing and grief! It blows a man up like a blad-
der. There's villainous news abroad. Here was Sir
John Bracy from your father. You must to the court
in the morning. That same mad fellow of the North,
Percy, and he of Wales that gave Amamon the bas-   340
tinado, and made Lucifer cuckold, and swore the
Devil his true liegeman upon the cross of a Welsh
hook—what a plague call you him?

Poins. Owen Glendower.

Fal. Owen, Owen—the same; and his son-in-law   345
Mortimer, and old Northumberland, and that spright-
ly Scot of Scots, Douglas, that runs a-horseback up a
hill perpendicular—

353. **rascal:** rascal deer, an inferior or under-developed specimen not likely to provide much of a chase for the hunter; **metal:** mettle; material. Both **metal** and **run** are used in two senses. He will stand firm both literally and figuratively.

361. **bluecaps:** Scots.

366. **civil buffeting hold:** domestic revolt continue.

A cuckold.
From a seventeenth-century ballad.

Prince. He that rides at high speed and with his
pistol kills a sparrow flying.   350

Fal. You have hit it.

Prince. So did he never the sparrow.

Fal. Well, that rascal hath good metal in him; he
will not run.

Prince. Why, what a rascal art thou then, to praise 355
him so for running!

Fal. A-horseback, ye cuckoo! but afoot he will not
budge a foot.

Prince. Yes, Jack, upon instinct.

Fal. I grant ye, upon instinct. Well, he is there too, 360
and one Mordake, and a thousand bluecaps more.
Worcester is stol'n away tonight; thy father's beard
is turned white with the news; you may buy land
now as cheap as stinking mack'rel.

Prince. Why then, it is like, if there come a hot 365
June, and this civil buffeting hold, we shall buy
maidenheads as they buy hobnails, by the hundreds.

Fal. By the mass, lad, thou sayest true; it is like we
shall have good trading that way. But tell me, Hal,
art not thou horrible afeard? Thou being heir appar- 370
ent, could the world pick thee out three such enemies again as that fiend Douglas, that spirit Percy,
and that devil Glendower? Art thou not horribly
afraid? Doth not thy blood thrill at it?

Prince. Not a whit, i' faith. I lack some of thy in- 375
stinct.

Fal. Well, thou wilt be horribly chid tomorrow
when thou comest to thy father. If thou love me,
practice an answer.

382. **state:** chair of state.

384. **joined-stool:** a stool made by a joiner—a practical but undistinguished piece of furniture.

391. **in King Cambyses' vein:** with the emotional raving characteristic of King Cambyses in Thomas Preston's drama *Cambyses, King of Persia* (1570).

392. **leg:** bow of homage, a necessary courtesy to the sovereign.

398. **convey:** help her hence; **tristful:** sad; tearful.

400-1. **harlotry:** an adjective indicating only good-natured familiarity.

402. **tickle-brain:** a slang word for liquor, hence also one who deals in it.

405-6. **For . . . grows:** a common proverb.

Prince. Do thou stand for my father and examine 380
me upon the particulars of my life.

Fal. Shall I? Content. This chair shall be my state,
this dagger my scepter, and this cushion my crown.

Prince. Thy state is taken for a joined-stool, thy
golden scepter for a leaden dagger, and thy precious 385
rich crown for a pitiful bald crown.

Fal. Well, an the fire of grace be not quite out of
thee, now shalt thou be moved. Give me a cup of
sack to make my eyes look red, that it may be
thought I have wept; for I must speak in passion, 390
and I will do it in King Cambyses' vein.

Prince. Well, here is my leg.

Fal. And here is my speech. Stand aside, nobility.

Hos. O Jesu, this is excellent sport, i' faith!

Fal. Weep not, sweet queen, for trickling tears are 395
vain.

Hos. O, the Father, how he holds his countenance!

Fal. For God's sake, lords, convey my tristful
queen! For tears do stop the floodgates of her eyes.

Hos. O Jesu, he doth it as like one of these har- 400
lotry players as ever I see!

Fal. Peace, good pintpot. Peace, good tickle-
brain.—Harry, I do not only marvel where thou
spendest thy time, but also how thou art accom-
panied. For though the camomile, the more it is 405
trodden on, the faster it grows, yet youth, the more
it is wasted, the sooner it wears. That thou art my
son I have partly thy mother's word, partly my own
opinion, but chiefly a villainous trick of thine eye
and a foolish hanging of thy nether lip that doth 410

411. **warrant:** assure.

413. **micher:** truant.

421. **not in pleasure, but in passion:** not in jest, but in sorrow.

427. **goodly:** good-looking; **portly:** dignified; stately.

432. **lewdly given:** inclined to baseness.

434. **peremptorily:** absolutely; without possibility of being contradicted.

warrant me. If then thou be son to me, here lies the
point: why, being son to me, art thou so pointed at?
Shall the blessed sun of heaven prove a micher and
eat blackberries? A question not to be asked. Shall
the son of England prove a thief and take purses? A   415
question to be asked. There is a thing, Harry, which
thou hast often heard of, and it is known to many in
our land by the name of pitch. This pitch, as ancient
writers do report, doth defile; so doth the company
thou keepest. For, Harry, now I do not speak to thee   420
in drink, but in tears; not in pleasure, but in passion;
not in words only, but in woes also: and yet there is
a virtuous man whom I have often noted in thy
company, but I know not his name.

Prince. What manner of man, an it like your   425
Majesty?

Fal. A goodly portly man, i' faith, and a corpu-
lent; of a cheerful look, a pleasing eye, and a most
noble carriage; and, as I think, his age some fifty,
or, by'r Lady, inclining to threescore; and now I re-   430
member me, his name is Falstaff. If that man should
be lewdly given, he deceiveth me; for, Harry, I see
virtue in his looks. If then the tree may be known by
the fruit, as the fruit by the tree, then, peremptorily
I speak it, there is virtue in that Falstaff. Him keep   435
with, the rest banish. And tell me now, thou naughty
varlet, tell me where hast thou been this month?

Prince. Dost thou speak like a king? Do thou stand
for me, and I'll play my father.

Fal. Depose me? If thou dost it half so gravely,   440
so majestically, both in word and matter, hang me

442-43. **rabbit-sucker:** suckling rabbit; **poulter's hare:** poulterer's hare; that is, one hanging in a poultry dealer's shop.

450. **tickle ye for a young prince:** play the Prince in good part.

451. **ungracious:** lacking grace; wicked.

455. **converse:** consort; keep company with.

456. **humors:** fluids, with the implication that they are unhealthy secretions; **bolting hutch:** a bin into which flour was sifted.

457. **bombard:** a leather container for drink; also a toper.

458-59. **Manningtree ox:** a prime beef carcass. Manningtree, Essex, was the site of annual fairs at which plays were performed and whole oxen roasted.

459-51. **Vice . . . Iniquity . . . Ruffian:** all traditional figures in morality plays. The Vice might sometimes be called "Iniquity" or by the name of some other specific sin such as "Vanity." **Ruffian** or "ruffin" was a slang term for the Devil; **Vanity in years:** i.e., old Vanity; elderly personification of worldliness.

462. **neat and cleanly:** precise and skillful.

463. **cunning:** clever.

466. **take me with you:** allow me to understand you.

up by the heels for a rabbit-sucker, or a poulter's
hare.

Prince. Well, here I am set.

Fal. And here I stand. Judge, my masters.   445

Prince. Now, Harry, whence come you?

Fal. My noble lord, from Eastcheap.

Prince. The complaints I hear of thee are grievous.

Fal. 'Sblood, my lord, they are false! [*Aside*] Nay,
I'll tickle ye for a young prince, i' faith.   450

Prince. Swearest thou, ungracious boy? Henceforth ne'er look on me. Thou art violently carried
away from grace. There is a devil haunts thee in the
likeness of an old fat man; a tun of man is thy companion. Why dost thou converse with that trunk of   455
humors, that bolting hutch of beastliness, that swoll'n
parcel of dropsies, that huge bombard of sack, that
stuffed cloakbag of guts, that roasted Manningtree
ox with the pudding in his belly, that reverend Vice,
that grey Iniquity, that father Ruffian, that Vanity   460
in years? Wherein is he good, but to taste sack and
drink it? wherein neat and cleanly, but to carve a
capon and eat it? wherein cunning, but in craft?
wherein crafty, but in villainy? wherein villainous,
but in all things? wherein worthy, but in nothing?   465

Fal. I would your Grace would take me with you.
Whom means your Grace?

Prince. That villainous abominable misleader of
youth, Falstaff, that old white-bearded Satan.

Fal. My lord, the man I know.   470

Prince. I know thou dost.

Fal. But to say I know more harm in him than in

475. **saving your reverence:** an apology for using the unpleasant word which follows. Such courtesy was conventional in speaking of evil or taboo subjects.

489. **watch:** company of watchmen.

493-94. **the Devil rides upon a fiddlestick:** here's a how-de-do. A proverbial expression.

myself were to say more than I know. That he is old
(the more the pity), his white hairs do witness it;
but that he is (saving your reverence) a whoremas-   475
ter, that I utterly deny. If sack and sugar be a fault,
God help the wicked! If to be old and merry be a
sin, then many an old host that I know is damned.
If to be fat be to be hated, then Pharaoh's lean kine
are to be loved. No, my good lord: banish Peto,   480
banish Bardolph, banish Poins; but for sweet Jack
Falstaff, kind Jack Falstaff, true Jack Falstaff, valiant
Jack Falstaff, and therefore more valiant being, as
he is, old Jack Falstaff, banish not him thy Harry's
company, banish not him thy Harry's company.   485
Banish plump Jack, and banish all the world!
   Prince. I do, I will.   [*A knocking heard.*]
      [*Exeunt Hostess, Francis, and Bardolph.*]

Enter *Bardolph*, running.

   Bar. O, my lord, my lord! the sheriff with a most
monstrous watch is at the door.
   Fal. Out, ye rogue! Play out the play. I have much   490
to say in the behalf of that Falstaff.

Enter the *Hostess*.

   Hos. O Jesu, my lord, my lord!
   Prince. Heigh, heigh, the Devil rides upon a fid-
dlestick! What's the matter?
   Hos. The sheriff and all the watch are at the door.   495

498-500. **Never . . . so:** This passage is obscure and scholars have argued over its meaning. Falstaff is alarmed that justice is at the door, as well as concerned at the serious turn their game has taken; he continues to urge the Prince not to forsake him.

502. **major:** major premise, with a pun on major/mayor, made possible by the similarity of pronunciation.

503. **so:** so be it; well and good; **cart:** i.e., to transport him to the gallows.

506. **arras:** a decorative hanging suspended from the wall.

509. **their date is out:** they have run their limit; are gone.

513. **hue and cry:** householders were supposed to take part in a **hue and cry** (serve as a posse) in pursuit of suspected criminals.

521. **engage:** pledge.

They are come to search the house. Shall I let them
in?

Fal. Dost thou hear, Hal? Never call a true piece
of gold a counterfeit. Thou art essentially mad without seeming so.   500

Prince. And thou a natural coward without instinct.

Fal. I deny your major. If you will deny the sheriff,
so; if not, let him enter. If I become not a cart as well
as another man, a plague on my bringing up! I hope
I shall as soon be strangled with a halter as another. 505

Prince. Go hide thee behind the arras. The rest
walk up above. Now, my masters, for a true face and
good conscience.

Fal. Both which I have had; but their date is out,
and therefore I'll hide me.   *Exit.* 510

Prince. Call in the sheriff.

                [*Exeunt all but the Prince and Peto.*]

          Enter *Sheriff* and the *Carrier*.

Now, master sheriff, what is your will with me?

Sher. First, pardon me, my lord. A hue and cry
Hath followed certain men unto this house.

Prince. What men?   515

Sher. One of them is well known, my gracious lord—
A gross fat man.

Car.   As fat as butter.

Prince. The man, I do assure you, is not here,
For I myself at this time have employed him.   520
And, sheriff, I will engage my word to thee
That I will by tomorrow dinnertime

533. **Paul's:** St. Paul's Cathedral, a noted land-
mark in London.

547. **ob.:** a halfpenny; an abbreviation for the
Greek *obolus*.

548. **monstrous:** extraordinary.

Send him to answer thee, or any man,
For anything he shall be charged withal;
And so let me entreat you leave the house.   525

Sher. I will, my lord. There are two gentlemen
Have in this robbery lost three hundred marks.

Prince. It may be so. If he have robbed these men,
He shall be answerable; and so farewell.

Sher. Good night, my noble lord.   530

Prince. I think it is good morrow, is it not?

Sher. Indeed, my lord, I think it be two o'clock.
                              Exit [*with Carrier*].

Prince. This oily rascal is known as well as Paul's.
Go call him forth.

Peto. Falstaff! Fast asleep behind the arras, and 535
snorting like a horse.

Prince. Hark how hard he fetches breath. Search
his pockets.
He searcheth his pockets and findeth certain papers.
What hast thou found?

Peto. Nothing but papers, my lord.   540

Prince. Let's see what they be. Read them.

Peto. [*Reads*] "Item, A capon . . . . . ii s. ii d.
                Item, Sauce . . . . . . iiii d.
                Item, Sack two gallons . v s. viii d.
                Item, Anchovies and   545
                   sack after supper . . ii s. vi d.
                Item, Bread . . . . . ob."

Prince. O monstrous! but one halfpennyworth of
bread to this intolerable deal of sack! What there is

550. **close:** safe; **at more advantage:** at a better opportunity.

553-54. **charge of foot:** command of a foot company.

555-56. **advantage:** addition; **betimes:** early.

A seventeenth-century windmill.
From T. F., *Divers Devises* (1592–1622).
(See III. i. 174.)

else, keep close; we'll read it at more advantage. 550
There let him sleep till day. I'll to the court in the
morning. We must all to the wars, and thy place shall
be honorable. I'll procure this fat rogue a charge of
foot, and I know his death will be a march of twelve
score. The money shall be paid back again with ad- 555
vantage. Be with me betimes in the morning, and so
good morrow, Peto.

Peto. Good morrow, good my lord.

Exeunt.

THE HISTORY OF
HENRY
THE FOURTH
[PART 1]

ACT III

III. i. Hotspur, Worcester, Mortimer, and Owen Glendower meet to complete their alliance. Hotspur is impatient at Glendower's boastful claims of magic power and mocks him. They agree, however, on the division of England into three parts for the Percies, Mortimer, and Glendower. Hotspur and Mortimer take leave of their wives and all prepare to ride as soon as the writing of their agreement is completed.

|||||||||||||||||||||||||||||||||||||||

2. **induction:** beginning; originally an introductory scene for a play; **prosperous hope:** hope of success.

9. **Lancaster:** King Henry.

15. **front:** forehead.

16. **cressets:** vessels holding combustible material to provide light, usually mounted on a tall stand or suspended from a high point.

ACT III

Scene I. [Bangor, Wales. The Archdeacon's house.]

Enter *Hotspur, Worcester, Lord Mortimer,*
Owen Glendower.

Mor. These promises are fair, the parties sure,
And our induction full of prosperous hope.
Hot. Lord Mortimer, and cousin Glendower,
Will you sit down?
And uncle Worcester. A plague upon it!   5
I have forgot the map.
Glen. No, here it is. Sit, cousin Percy;
Sit, good cousin Hotspur, for by that name
As oft as Lancaster doth speak of you,
His cheek looks pale, and with a rising sigh   10
He wisheth you in heaven.
Hot. And you in hell, as oft as he hears Owen
Glendower spoke of.
Glen. I cannot blame him. At my nativity
The front of heaven was full of fiery shapes   15
Of burning cressets, and at my birth
The frame and huge foundation of the earth
Shaked like a coward.
Hot. Why, so it would have done at the same sea-

34. **enlargement:** freedom.
35. **beldame:** aged woman.
37. **distemp'rature:** disorder.
38. **passion:** great distress; see II. iv. 421.
48. **clipped in with:** encompassed by.
49. **chides:** contends loudly with; beats against.
50. **read to me:** given me lessons.

son if your mother's cat had but kittened, though   20
yourself had never been born.

   Glen. I say the earth did shake when I was born.

   Hot. And I say the earth was not of my mind,
If you suppose as fearing you it shook.

   Glen. The heavens were all on fire, the earth did   25
    tremble.

   Hot. O, then the earth shook to see the heavens on
    fire,
And not in fear of your nativity.
Diseased nature oftentimes breaks forth   30
In strange eruptions; oft the teeming earth
Is with a kind of colic pinched and vexed
By the imprisoning of unruly wind
Within her womb, which, for enlargement striving,
Shakes the old beldame earth and topples down   35
Steeples and mossgrown towers. At your birth
Our grandam earth, having this distemp'rature,
In passion shook.

   Glen.   Cousin, of many men
I do not bear these crossings. Give me leave   40
To tell you once again that at my birth
The front of heaven was full of fiery shapes,
The goats ran from the mountains, and the herds
Were strangely clamorous to the frighted fields.
These signs have marked me extraordinary,   45
And all the courses of my life do show
I am not in the roll of common men.
Where is he living, clipped in with the sea
That chides the banks of England, Scotland, Wales,
Which calls me pupil or hath read to me?   50

52. **trace me:** follow closely; that is, come near to equaling; **tedious:** painful; **art:** magic.

53. **hold me pace:** keep pace with me; **deep:** occult.

54. **speaks better Welsh:** Hotspur is bored with Glendower and the best he can say of him is that he speaks good Welsh (which is small credit for a native Welshman). He may also mean that he is a braggart.

57. **vasty deep:** limitless infernal regions.

70-1. **made head:** raised an army; see I. iii. 301.

74. **Bootless:** profitlessly.

78. **right:** territory rightfully claimed.

79. **our threefold order ta'en:** the division into three parts on which we have agreed.

And bring him out that is but woman's son
Can trace me in the tedious ways of art
And hold me pace in deep experiments.

Hot. I think there's no man speaks better Welsh.
I'll to dinner.   55

Mor. Peace, cousin Percy; you will make him mad.

Glen. I can call spirits from the vasty deep.

Hot. Why, so can I, or so can any man;
But will they come when you do call for them?

Glen. Why, I can teach you, cousin, to command   60
the Devil.

Hot. And I can teach thee, coz, to shame the
  Devil—
By telling truth. Tell truth and shame the Devil.
If thou have power to raise him, bring him hither,   65
And I'll be sworn I have power to shame him hence.
O, while you live, tell truth and shame the Devil!

Mor. Come, come, no more of this unprofitable
chat.

Glen. Three times hath Harry Bolingbroke made   70
  head
Against my power; thrice from the banks of Wye
And sandy-bottomed Severn have I sent him
Bootless home and weather-beaten back.

Hot. Home without boots, and in foul weather too?   75
How 'scapes he agues, in the Devil's name?

Glen. Come, here is the map. Shall we divide our
  right
According to our threefold order ta'en?

Mor. The Archdeacon hath divided it   80
Into three limits very equally.

82. **hitherto:** hence; that is, to this point.

87. **lying off from:** beginning at.

88. **indentures tripartite:** contracts in triplicate.

89. **sealed interchangeably:** that is, signed by each party to the agreement.

95. **father:** father-in-law; a common usage.

101. **conduct:** escort.

105. **moiety:** portion.

107. **cranking:** twisting.

109. **cantle:** section.

111. **smug:** trim.

112. **fair and evenly:** smoothly and straightly.

England, from Trent and Severn hitherto,
By south and east is to my part assigned;
All westward, Wales beyond the Severn shore,
And all the fertile land within that bound,   85
To Owen Glendower; and, dear coz, to you
The remnant northward lying off from Trent.
And our indentures tripartite are drawn,
Which being sealed interchangeably
(A business that this night may execute),   90
Tomorrow, cousin Percy, you and I
And my good Lord of Worcester will set forth
To meet your father and the Scottish power,
As is appointed us, at Shrewsbury.
My father Glendower is not ready yet,   95
Nor shall we need his help these fourteen days.
[*To Glendower*] Within that space you may have
      drawn together
Your tenants, friends, and neighboring gentlemen.
    Glen. A shorter time shall send me to you, lords;   100
And in my conduct shall your ladies come,
From whom you now must steal and take no leave,
For there will be a world of water shed
Upon the parting of your wives and you.
    Hot. Methinks my moiety, north from Burton here,   105
In quantity equals not one of yours.
See how this river comes me cranking in
And cuts me from the best of all my land
A huge half-moon, a monstrous cantle out.
I'll have the current in this place dammed up,   110
And here the smug and silver Trent shall run
In a new channel fair and evenly.

114. **bottom:** bottom land of the river.

119. **Gelding the opposed continent:** cutting into the opposite shore line.

121. **charge:** expense; i.e., a new channel can be dug for little cost.

136. **gave the tongue a helpful ornament:** embellished the English language by the lyrics he composed.

137. **virtue:** excellence.

140. **meter ballet-mongers:** rhymesters.

141. **canstick:** candlestick.

It shall not wind with such a deep indent
To rob me of so rich a bottom here.
   Glen. Not wind? It shall, it must! You see it doth. 115
   Mor. Yea, but
Mark how he bears his course, and runs me up
With like advantage on the other side,
Gelding the opposed continent as much
As on the other side it takes from you.   120
   Wor. Yea, but a little charge will trench him here
And on this north side win this cape of land;
And then he runs straight and even.
   Hot. I'll have it so. A little charge will do it.
   Glen. I will not have it alt'red.   125
   Hot.   Will not you?
   Glen. No, nor you shall not.
   Hot.   Who shall say me nay?
   Glen. Why, that will I.
   Hot. Let me not understand you then; speak it in 130
   Welsh.
   Glen. I can speak English, lord, as well as you;
For I was trained up in the English court,
Where, being but young, I framed to the harp
Many an English ditty lovely well,   135
And gave the tongue a helpful ornament—
A virtue that was never seen in you.
   Hot. Marry, and I am glad of it with all my heart!
I had rather be a kitten and cry mew
Than one of these same meter ballet-mongers.   140
I had rather hear a brazen canstick turned
Or a dry wheel grate on the axletree,
And that would set my teeth nothing on edge,

155. **Break with:** i.e., break the news to.

160. **moldwarp:** literally, "earth-thrower"; i.e., the mole, who breaks the even surface of the soil.

161. **Merlin:** a magician famous in the Arthurian legends.

163. **griffin:** a fabulous animal, half lion, half eagle; **molten:** molted.

164. **couching:** crouching; **ramping:** rearing.

165. **skimble-skamble:** scrambled; nonsensical.

169-70. **go to:** is that so; a comment forced from Hotspur by an effort to be courteous even though he was bored.

172. **railing:** scolding.

A griffin.
From Giulio Cesare Capaccio, *Delle imprese trattato* (1592).

Nothing so much as mincing poetry:
'Tis like the forced gait of a shuffling nag.   145
  Glen. Come, you shall have Trent turned.
  Hot. I do not care. I'll give thrice so much land
To any well-deserving friend;
But in the way of bargain, mark ye me,
I'll cavil on the ninth part of a hair.   150
Are the indentures drawn? Shall we be gone?
  Glen. The moon shines fair; you may away by
    night.
I'll haste the writer, and withal
Break with your wives of your departure hence.   155
I am afraid my daughter will run mad,
So much she doteth on her Mortimer.   *Exit.*
  Mor. Fie, cousin Percy! how you cross my father!
  Hot. I cannot choose. Sometimes he angers me
With telling me of the moldwarp and the ant,   160
Of the dreamer Merlin and his prophecies,
And of a dragon and a finless fish,
A clip-winged griffin and a molten raven,
A couching lion and a ramping cat,
And such a deal of skimble-skamble stuff   165
As puts me from my faith. I tell you what—
He held me last night at least nine hours
In reckoning up the several devils' names
That were his lackeys. I cried "hum," and "Well, go
    to!"   170
But marked him not a word. O, he is as tedious
As a tired horse, a railing wife;
Worse than a smoky house. I had rather live

175. **cates:** dainties; originally purchased, as contrasted with home-grown, foods.

178. **profited:** proficient.

179. **concealments:** mysteries; magical secrets.

184. **come 'cross his humor:** disagree with him.

186. **tempted:** tried (his patience).

187. **danger and reproof:** dangerous reproof.

189. **willful-blame:** blameable for your willfulness.

191. **besides:** beyond.

193. **blood:** mettle; fiery spirit.

194. **dearest grace:** highest honor.

195. **present:** display.

196. **want of government:** lack of self-control.

197. **opinion:** self-conceit.

200. **parts:** qualities or accomplishments.

201. **Beguiling:** cheating.

202-3. **I am schooled:** I have had quite a lesson!; **be your speed:** cause you to prosper.

With cheese and garlic in a windmill far
Than feed on cates and have him talk to me   175
In any summerhouse in Christendom.

  Mor. In faith, he is a worthy gentleman,
Exceedingly well read, and profited
In strange concealments, valiant as a lion,
And wondrous affable, and as bountiful   180
As mines of India. Shall I tell you, cousin?
He holds your temper in a high respect
And curbs himself even of his natural scope
When you come 'cross his humor. Faith, he does.
I warrant you that man is not alive   185
Might so have tempted him as you have done
Without the taste of danger and reproof.
But do not use it oft, let me entreat you.

  Wor. In faith, my lord, you are too willful-blame,
And since your coming hither have done enough   190
To put him quite besides his patience.
You must needs learn, lord, to amend this fault.
Though sometimes it show greatness, courage, blood—
And that's the dearest grace it renders you—
Yet oftentimes it doth present harsh rage,   195
Defect of manners, want of government,
Pride, haughtiness, opinion, and disdain;
The least of which haunting a nobleman
Loseth men's hearts, and leaves behind a stain
Upon the beauty of all parts besides,   200
Beguiling them of commendation.

  Hot. Well, I am schooled. Good manners be your
    speed!
Here come our wives, and let us take our leave.

205. **spite:** annoyance.

213. **desperate:** recklessly determined; **here:** about this matter; **peevish:** obstinate.

214. **harlotry:** i.e., wench, not harlot; see II. iv. 400-1.

216. **That pretty Welsh:** that is, her tears.

219-20. **but for shame,/In such a parley should I answer thee:** that is, were it not unmanly to weep, I should answer you in the same language.

222. **feeling disputation:** affecting (stirring) discourse.

227. **division:** melody.

Enter Glendower with the Ladies.

Mor. This is the deadly spite that angers me—   205
My wife can speak no English, I no Welsh.
　Glen. My daughter weeps; she will not part with
　　you;
She'll be a soldier too, she'll to the wars.
　Mor. Good father, tell her that she and my aunt 210
　　Percy
Shall follow in your conduct speedily.
　　　　*Glendower speaks to her in Welsh, and she
　　　　　　　　answers him in the same.*
　Glen. She is desperate here. A peevish self-willed
　　harlotry,
One that no persuasion can do good upon.   215
　　　　　　　The Lady speaks in Welsh.
　Mor. I understand thy looks. That pretty Welsh
Which thou pourest down from these swelling
　　heavens
I am too perfect in; and, but for shame,
In such a parley should I answer thee.   220
　　　　　　　The Lady again in Welsh.
I understand thy kisses, and thou mine,
And that's a feeling disputation.
But I will never be a truant, love,
Till I have learnt thy language; for thy tongue
Makes Welsh as sweet as ditties highly penned,   225
Sung by a fair queen in a summer's bow'r,
With ravishing division, to her lute.
　Glen. Nay, if you melt, then will she run mad.
　　　　　　The Lady speaks again in Welsh.

230. **wanton rushes:** plentiful rushes. Rushes were in common use for floor coverings instead of rugs.

234. **crown the god of sleep:** i.e., give sleep the mastery of you.

235. **blood:** senses; **heaviness:** drowsiness.

238. **heavenly-harnessed team:** the horses of the sun god's chariot.

241. **our book:** the tripartite indenture; see lines 88-90.

243-45. **those musicians that shall play to you/Hang in the air a thousand leagues from hence,/And straight they shall be here:** Glendower promises to bring forth musicians from the air by magic.

251. **humorous:** full of odd moods.

254. **humors:** whimsical moods; see II. iv. 94.

256. **brach:** bitch.

Mor. O, I am ignorance itself in this!

Glen. She bids you on the wanton rushes lay you   230
down

And rest your gentle head upon her lap,
And she will sing the song that pleaseth you
And on your eyelids crown the god of sleep,
Charming your blood with pleasing heaviness,   235
Making such difference 'twixt wake and sleep
As is the difference betwixt day and night
The hour before the heavenly-harnessed team
Begins his golden progress in the east.

Mor. With all my heart I'll sit and hear her sing.   240
By that time will our book, I think, be drawn.

Glen. Do so,
And those musicians that shall play to you
Hang in the air a thousand leagues from hence,
And straight they shall be here. Sit, and attend.   245

Hot. Come, Kate, thou art perfect in lying down.
Come, quick, quick, that I may lay my head in thy
lap.

Lady P. Go, ye giddy goose.   *The music plays.*

Hot. Now I perceive the Devil understands Welsh;   250
And 'tis no marvel, he is so humorous.
By'r Lady, he is a good musician.

Lady P. Then should you be nothing but musical,
for you are altogether governed by humors. Lie still,
ye thief, and hear the lady sing in Welsh.   255

Hot. I had rather hear Lady, my brach, howl in
Irish.

Lady P. Wouldst thou have thy head broken?

Hot. No.

261. **'Tis a woman's fault:** no, I will be perverse, like a woman.

267. **sooth:** truth.

269. **comfit-maker's:** confectioner's.

272. **sarcenet:** a variety of thin, soft silk; i.e., insubstantial.

273. **Finsbury:** Finsbury Fields, a popular recreation area north of London.

276. **protest of pepper gingerbread:** spicecake oaths; that is, dainty and fragile swearing.

277. **velvet guards:** i.e., women of a class to think themselves fine because they have velvet guarding (braid) on their garments; **Sunday citizens:** citizens on their Sunday behavior.

280-81. **'Tis the next way to turn tailor or be redbreast-teacher:** Hotspur is contemptuous of music and disdains rhymers and singers; he would not want his wife to sing like a tailor or waste time teaching her bird to sing.

286. **this:** this time.

Lady P. Then be still.   260

Hot. Neither! 'Tis a woman's fault.

Lady P. Now God help thee!

Hot. To the Welsh lady's bed.

Lady P. What's that?

Hot. Peace! she sings.   265

    Here the Lady sings a Welsh song.

Come, Kate, I'll have your song too.

Lady P. Not mine, in good sooth.

Hot. Not yours, in good sooth? Heart! you swear
like a comfit-maker's wife. "Not you, in good sooth!"
and "as true as I live!" and "as God shall mend me!"   270
and "as sure as day!"

And givest such sarcenet surety for thy oaths
As if thou never walkst further than Finsbury.
Swear me, Kate, like a lady as thou art,
A good mouth-filling oath, and leave "in sooth"   275
And such protest of pepper gingerbread
To velvet guards and Sunday citizens.
Come, sing.

Lady P. I will not sing.

Hot. 'Tis the next way to turn tailor or be red-   280
breast-teacher. An the indentures be drawn, I'll away
within these two hours; and so come in when ye
will.   *Exit.*

Glen. Come, come, Lord Mortimer. You are as slow
As hot Lord Percy is on fire to go.   285
By this our book is drawn; we'll but seal,
And then to horse immediately.

Mor.   With all my heart.

        Exeunt.

III. ii. King Henry, reproaching Prince Henry for his wildness and the shame he has brought upon his father, compares his public behavior with that of the deposed Richard II. The King declares that he himself won respect and reverence from the populace because he had kept himself remote. Hal denies that he is guilty of all the misdeeds imputed to him and swears that in battle he will earn the military glory that now enhances Hotspur's reputation.

Word is received that the English rebels have combined with the Scots at Shrewsbury, and the King gives orders to set forth against the enemy.

⸻

10. **passages of life:** i.e., the course of life which you follow.

11-2. **marked/For:** intended to be.

14. **inordinate:** disorderly; improper for one of his position.

15. **lewd:** base; see II. iv. 432; **attempts:** pursuits.

17. **matched:** associated; **grafted to:** unnaturally joined to.

19. **hold their level:** accord.

21. **Quit:** acquit myself of.

24. **extenuation:** forgiveness.

Scene II. [London. The palace.]

Enter the *King*, *Prince of Wales*, and *others*.

King. Lords, give us leave: the Prince of Wales
    and I
Must have some private conference; but be near at
    hand,
For we shall presently have need of you.   5
                              Exeunt Lords.
I know not whether God will have it so
For some displeasing service I have done,
That, in his secret doom, out of my blood
He'll breed revengement and a scourge for me;
But thou dost in thy passages of life   10
Make me believe that thou art only marked
For the hot vengeance and the rod of heaven
To punish my mistreadings. Tell me else,
Could such inordinate and low desires,
Such poor, such bare, such lewd, such mean attempts, 15
Such barren pleasures, rude society,
As thou art matched withal and grafted to,
Accompany the greatness of thy blood
And hold their level with thy princely heart?
    Prince. So please your Majesty, I would I could   20
Quit all offenses with as clear excuse
As well as I am doubtless I can purge
Myself of many I am charged withal.
Yet such extenuation let me beg
As, in reproof of many tales devised,   25

27. **pickthanks:** persons who tell tales in order to curry favor with the great.

30. **submission:** confession.

32. **affections:** inclinations; **hold a wing:** i.e., fly a course.

33. **from:** opposite from.

34. **rudely:** that is, because of your violence. The Prince was dismissed from the council, according to Holinshed, because he struck the Chief Justice for imprisoning one of his friends.

42. **common-hackneyed in the eyes of men:** common to everyone. The contemptuous term comes from the hackney horses for common hire.

44-5. **Opinion, that did help me to the crown,/ Had still kept loyal to possession:** popular opinion, which supported my seizure of the crown, would have remained loyal to the King, Richard II.

52. **stole all courtesy from heaven:** assumed a saintly modesty.

Which oft the ear of greatness needs must hear
By smiling pickthanks and base newsmongers,
I may, for some things true wherein my youth
Hath faulty wand'red and irregular,
Find pardon on my true submission.   30
    King. God pardon thee! Yet let me wonder, Harry,
At thy affections, which do hold a wing
Quite from the flight of all thy ancestors.
Thy place in council thou hast rudely lost,
Which by thy younger brother is supplied,   35
And art almost an alien to the hearts
Of all the court and princes of my blood.
The hope and expectation of thy time
Is ruined, and the soul of every man
Prophetically do forethink thy fall.   40
Had I so lavish of my presence been,
So common-hackneyed in the eyes of men,
So stale and cheap to vulgar company,
Opinion, that did help me to the crown,
Had still kept loyal to possession   45
And left me in reputeless banishment,
A fellow of no mark nor likelihood.
By being seldom seen, I could not stir
But, like a comet, I was wond'red at;
That men would tell their children, "This is he!"   50
Others would say, "Where? Which is Bolingbroke?"
And then I stole all courtesy from heaven,
And dressed myself in such humility
That I did pluck allegiance from men's hearts,
Loud shouts and salutations from their mouths   55
Even in the presence of the crowned King.

59. **state:** state pomp; full regalia of majesty.

60. **showed:** appeared.

61. **solemnity:** special quality, as of a ceremonial occasion.

62. **skipping:** frivolous.

63. **rash bavin:** quickly kindled and as soon consumed, as the next line makes clear. A **bavin** is a bundle of brushwood.

64. **carded:** debased. The Elizabethans used the word "card" to mean mixing drinks of varying quality. Its derivation in this sense is obscure.

66. **their scorns:** i.e., the scorn of the populace for fools.

67-8. **gave his countenance, against his name,/ To laugh at gibing boys:** gave his approval, to the detriment of his reputation, to gibing boys. There is probably a pun on countenance, meaning both "face" and "authority" or "approval"; **stand the push:** endure the jostling.

69. **beardless vain comparative:** youthful and foolish satirist; see **comparative** at I. ii. 82.

71. **Enfeoffed:** gave himself entirely. **Enfeoffed** is a legal term meaning to convey absolutely; **popularity:** association with the populace.

79. **community:** frequence of communion; that is, the fact that seeing him was no rarity.

84. **rend'red such aspect:** gave him such glances.

85. **cloudy:** lowering with anger; frowning.

87. **line:** position; see I. iii. 177.

Thus did I keep my person fresh and new,
My presence, like a robe pontifical,
Ne'er seen but wond'red at; and so my state,
Seldom but sumptuous, showed like a feast   60
And won by rareness such solemnity.
The skipping King, he ambled up and down
With shallow jesters and rash bavin wits,
Soon kindled and soon burnt; carded his state;
Mingled his royalty with capering fools;   65
Had his great name profaned with their scorns
And gave his countenance, against his name,
To laugh at gibing boys and stand the push
Of every beardless vain comparative;
Grew a companion to the common streets,   70
Enfeoffed himself to popularity;
That, being daily swallowed by men's eyes,
They surfeited with honey and began
To loathe the taste of sweetness, whereof a little
More than a little is by much too much.   75
So, when he had occasion to be seen,
He was but as the cuckoo is in June,
Heard, not regarded—seen, but with such eyes
As, sick and blunted with community,
Afford no extraordinary gaze,   80
Such as is bent on sunlike majesty
When it shines seldom in admiring eyes;
But rather drowsed and hung their eyelids down,
Slept in his face, and rend'red such aspect
As cloudy men use to their adversaries,   85
Being with his presence glutted, gorged, and full.
And in that very line, Harry, standest thou;

89. **vile participation:** base association.

94. **thrice-gracious:** thrice is used vaguely here to mean "very," "extremely."

100. **to boot:** in addition.

101. **interest:** legal right.

102. **shadow of succession:** immediate heir apparent.

103. **color:** semblance; false appearance.

104. **harness:** armored men.

105. **Turns head:** directs an army; **the lion's:** i.e., the King's. The lion was, and is, a symbol of English sovereignty.

106. **no more in debt to years:** see note at I. i. 88-92 for comment on Hotspur's age.

112-13. **Holds from all soldiers chief majority/And military title capital:** is awarded by all soldiers the greatest eminence and the highest martial title.

115. **swathling:** swaddling.

118. **Enlarged:** freed; see III. i. 34.

For thou hast lost thy princely privilege
With vile participation. Not an eye
But is aweary of thy common sight,   90
Save mine, which hath desired to see thee more;
Which now doth that I would not have it do—
Make blind itself with foolish tenderness.
    Prince. I shall hereafter, my thrice-gracious lord,
Be more myself.   95
    King.   For all the world,
As thou art to this hour was Richard then
When I from France set foot at Ravenspurgh;
And even as I was then is Percy now.
Now, by my scepter, and my soul to boot,   100
He hath more worthy interest to the state
Than thou, the shadow of succession;
For of no right, nor color like to right,
He doth fill fields with harness in the realm,
Turns head against the lion's armed jaws,   105
And, being no more in debt to years than thou,
Leads ancient lords and reverend bishops on
To bloody battles and to bruising arms.
What never-dying honor hath he got
Against renowned Douglas! whose high deeds,   110
Whose hot incursions and great name in arms
Holds from all soldiers chief majority
And military title capital
Through all the kingdoms that acknowledge Christ.
Thrice hath this Hotspur, Mars in swathling clothes, 115
This infant warrior, in his enterprises
Discomfited great Douglas; ta'en him once,
Enlarged him, and made a friend of him,

119. **fill the mouth of deep defiance up:** i.e., make the greatest possible show of defiance.

123. **Capitulate:** bind themselves by articles of agreement; **up:** up in arms.

127. **vassal:** ignoble.

128. **start of spleen:** prompting of irrational impulse; see **spleen** at II. iii. 83.

135. **redeem all this on Percy's head:** make up for the reputation I have at Percy's expense.

139. **favors:** features.

144. **unthought-of:** unvalued.

149. **indignities:** present lack of dignity.

To fill the mouth of deep defiance up
And shake the peace and safety of our throne.   120
And what say you to this? Percy, Northumberland,
The Archbishop's Grace of York, Douglas, Mortimer
Capitulate against us and are up.
But wherefore do I tell these news to thee?
Why, Harry, do I tell thee of my foes,   125
Which art my nearest and dearest enemy?
Thou that art like enough, through vassal fear,
Base inclination, and the start of spleen,
To fight against me under Percy's pay,
To dog his heels and curtsy at his frowns,   130
To show how much thou art degenerate.
    Prince. Do not think so. You shall not find it so.
And God forgive them that so much have swayed
Your Majesty's good thoughts away from me.
I will redeem all this on Percy's head   135
And, in the closing of some glorious day,
Be bold to tell you that I am your son,
When I will wear a garment all of blood,
And stain my favors in a bloody mask,
Which, washed away, shall scour my shame with it.   140
And that shall be the day, whene'er it lights,
That this same child of honor and renown,
This gallant Hotspur, this all-praised knight,
And your unthought-of Harry chance to meet.
For every honor sitting on his helm,   145
Would they were multitudes, and on my head
My shames redoubled! For the time will come
That I shall make this northern youth exchange
His glorious deeds for my indignities.

150. **factor:** agent.

151. **engross up:** buy in quantity (with intent to monopolize the supply).

154. **worship:** honor.

159. **intemperance:** misbehavior.

160. **bands:** bonds.

162. **parcel:** portion; see II. iv. 103.

163. **A hundred thousand rebels die in this:** your resolution is sufficient to wipe out a hundred thousand rebels.

164. **charge:** command; **sovereign trust:** powerful responsibility.

166. **So hath the business:** i.e., the business requires speed.

167. **Lord Mortimer of Scotland:** really the Scottish Earl of March. Shakespeare has given him the name of the English Mortimers, who were also Earls of March.

175. **advertisement:** information.

Percy is but my factor, good my lord,　　　　　　150
To engross up glorious deeds on my behalf;
And I will call him to so strict account
That he shall render every glory up,
Yea, even the slightest worship of his time,
Or I will tear the reckoning from his heart.　　　155
This in the name of God I promise here;
The which if He be pleased I shall perform,
I do beseech your Majesty may salve
The long-grown wounds of my intemperance.
If not, the end of life cancels all bands,　　　　160
And I will die a hundred thousand deaths
Ere break the smallest parcel of this vow.
　　King. A hundred thousand rebels die in this!
Thou shalt have charge and sovereign trust herein.

Enter *Blunt.*

How now, good Blunt? Thy looks are full of speed.　165
　　Blunt. So hath the business that I come to speak of.
Lord Mortimer of Scotland hath sent word
That Douglas and the English rebels met
The eleventh of this month at Shrewsbury.
A mighty and a fearful head they are,　　　　　170
If promises be kept on every hand,
As ever off'red foul play in a state.
　　King. The Earl of Westmoreland set forth today;
With him my son, Lord John of Lancaster;
For this advertisement is five days old.　　　　175
On Wednesday next, Harry, you shall set forward;
On Thursday we ourselves will march. Our meeting

180. **Our business valued**: weighing the time necessary for our business.

183. **Advantage feeds him fat while men delay**: we lose the edge of opportunity by delay.

⸻

III. iii. Falstaff pretends that the sweat and struggle at Gad's Hill have taken a sad toll of his flesh, and Bardolph agrees that he has fallen off somewhat. Falstaff charges Mistress Quickly with having picked his pocket, but the Prince enters and proves him a liar in saying that his pocket contained money. He informs Falstaff of his military command and sends Bardolph with messages to his brother John and Westmoreland.

⸻

2. **bate**: abate; shrink.

3-4. **loose gown**: a loose-fitting gown worn over street clothes or as a dressing gown; **applejohn**: an apple which improves in flavor by being dried.

5-6. **in some liking**: that is, still fairly sound of constitution.

9. **peppercorn, a brewer's horse**: two additional objects which are shriveled and look past their prime. In Elizabethan times, horses unfit for other work were sold to brewers to be used as dray horses.

Is Bridgenorth; and, Harry, you shall march
Through Gloucestershire; by which account,
Our business valued, some twelve days hence   180
Our general forces at Bridgenorth shall meet.
Our hands are full of business. Let's away:
Advantage feeds him fat while men delay.

                                        Exeunt.

Scene III. [London. The Boar's Head Tavern.]

Enter *Falstaff* and *Bardolph.*

Fal. Bardolph, am I not fall'n away vilely since
this last action? Do I not bate? Do I not dwindle?
Why, my skin hangs about me like an old lady's loose
gown! I am withered like an old applejohn. Well,
I'll repent, and that suddenly, while I am in some   5
liking. I shall be out of heart shortly, and then I
shall have no strength to repent. An I have not forgotten what the inside of a church is made of, I am
a peppercorn, a brewer's horse. The inside of a
church! Company, villainous company, hath been   10
the spoil of me.

Bar. Sir John, you are so fretful you cannot live
long.

Fal. Why, there is it! Come, sing me a bawdy
song; make me merry. I was as virtuously given as   15
a gentleman need to be, virtuous enough: swore little,
diced not above seven times a week, went to a bawdy
house not above once in a quarter of an hour, paid

20. in good compass: in an orderly fashion.

26. admiral: flagship.

31-2. memento mori: a remembrance of death. Falstaff probably refers to a ring with a skull and crossbones. Such rings were frequently worn as a sign of mourning.

33. Dives: a reference to the Biblical story, see Luke 16:19–31.

36. By this fire, that's God's angel: a recollection of Psalms 104:4.

37. given over: that is, to evil ways.

40-1. ignis fatuus: will-o'-the-wisp.

42. triumph: illuminated spectacle.

44. links: small torches. Since streets were not uniformly lit, those out after dark often had to hire boys to light their way home with torches.

48. salamander: a lizard believed to thrive in fire. Falstaff is referring to Bardolph's nose.

A salamander.

From Horus Appollon, *De sacris notis et sculpturis* (1551).

money that I borrowed three or four times, lived
well, and in good compass; and now I live out of all   20
order, out of all compass.

Bar. Why, you are so fat, Sir John, that you must
needs be out of all compass—out of all reasonable
compass, Sir John.

Fal. Do thou amend thy face, and I'll amend my   25
life. Thou art our admiral, thou bearest the lantern
in the poop—but 'tis in the nose of thee. Thou art
the Knight of the Burning Lamp.

Bar. Why, Sir John, my face does you no harm.

Fal. No, I'll be sworn. I make as good use of it as   30
many a man doth of a death's-head or a memento
mori. I never see thy face but I think upon hellfire
and Dives that lived in purple; for there he is in his
robes, burning, burning. If thou wert any way given
to virtue, I would swear by thy face; my oath should   35
be "By this fire, that's God's angel." But thou art
altogether given over, and wert indeed, but for the
light in thy face, the son of utter darkness. When
thou ranst up Gad's Hill in the night to catch my
horse, if I did not think thou hadst been an ignis   40
fatuus or a ball of wildfire, there's no purchase in
money. O, thou art a perpetual triumph, an ever-
lasting bonfire-light! Thou hast saved me a thousand
marks in links and torches, walking with thee in the
night betwixt tavern and tavern; but the sack that   45
thou hast drunk me would have bought me lights as
good cheap at the dearest chandler's in Europe. I
have maintained that salamander of yours with fire

51. **I would my face were in your belly:** a common rebuke to a speaker who lingered too long on some topic, in this case, Bardolph's nose. Bardolph also gets in a dig at Falstaff's bulk.

52. **God-a-mercy:** God have mercy!

54. **Dame Partlet:** Pertelote, the hen in Chaucer's "Nun's Priest's Tale."

59. **tithe:** tenth part.

71. **Dowlas:** linen of a coarse weave.

72. **bolters:** sieves; see **bolting hutch;** II. iv. 456.

73. **holland:** a fine linen.

75. **by-drinkings:** drinks at odd times other than with meals.

An admiral with a lantern in the poop.

From Robert Farley, *Lychnocausia sive moralia facum emblemata* (1638).

any time this two-and-thirty years. God reward me
for it!   50

   Bar. 'Sblood, I would my face were in your belly!

   Fal. God-a-mercy! so should I be sure to be heart-
burned.

Enter *Hostess.*

How now, Dame Partlet the hen? Have you inquired
yet who picked my pocket?   55

   Hos. Why, Sir John, what do you think, Sir John?
Do you think I keep thieves in my house? I have
searched, I have inquired, so has my husband, man
by man, boy by boy, servant by servant. The tithe of
a hair was never lost in my house before.   60

   Fal. Ye lie, hostess. Bardolph was shaved and lost
many a hair, and I'll be sworn my pocket was picked.
Go to, you are a woman, go!

   Hos. Who, I? No; I defy thee! God's light, I was
never called so in mine own house before!   65

   Fal. Go to, I know you well enough.

   Hos. No, Sir John; you do not know me, Sir John.
I know you, Sir John. You owe me money, Sir John,
and now you pick a quarrel to beguile me of it. I
bought you a dozen of shirts to your back.   70

   Fal. Dowlas, filthy dowlas! I have given them away
to bakers' wives; they have made bolters of them.

   Hos. Now, as I am a true woman, holland of eight
shillings an ell. You owe money here besides, Sir
John, for your diet and by-drinkings, and money lent   75
you, four-and-twenty pound.

81. denier: a small French coin worth one-twelfth of a sou.

82. younker: youngster; greenhorn.

87. sneak-up: sneak.

S.D. after l. 89. truncheon: a short rod or staff, carried mainly by military officers.

90. Is the wind in that door: is that the way the wind blows?

92. two and two, Newgate fashion: that is, like fettered prisoners in Newgate Prison.

A fairly hearty-looking brewer's horse at Gracechurch Market. From Hugh Alley, *A Caveat for the City of London* (1598). (See III. iii. 9.)

76

Fal. He had his part of it; let him pay.

Hos. He? Alas, he is poor; he hath nothing.

Fal. How? Poor? Look upon his face. What call
you rich? Let them coin his nose, let them coin his   80
cheeks. I'll not pay a denier. What, will you make a
younker of me? Shall I not take mine ease in mine
inn but I shall have my pocket picked? I have lost a
seal-ring of my grandfather's worth forty mark.

Hos. O Jesu, I have heard the Prince tell him, I   85
know not how oft, that that ring was copper!

Fal. How? the Prince is a Jack, a sneak-up. 'Sblood,
an he were here, I would cudgel him like a dog if he
would say so.

> Enter the *Prince* [and *Peto*], marching, and
> *Falstaff* meets them, playing upon his
> truncheon like a fife.

How now, lad? Is the wind in that door, i' faith?   90
Must we all march?

Bar. Yea, two and two, Newgate fashion.

Hos. My lord, I pray you hear me.

Prince. What sayst thou, Mistress Quickly? How
doth thy husband? I love him well; he is an honest   95
man.

Hos. Good my lord, hear me.

Fal. Prithee let her alone and list to me.

Prince. What sayst thou, Jack?

Fal. The other night I fell asleep here behind the   100
arras and had my pocket picked. This house is turned
bawdy house; they pick pockets.

115-18. **no more faith . . . than in a stewed prune:** stewed prunes were commonly served in bawdy houses. They were thought to be a preventive of venereal disease; **a drawn fox:** that is, a fox forced from his lair for sport. His desire to escape death naturally makes him exert every effort of cunning and deceit; **for womanhood, Maid Marian may be the deputy's wife of the ward to thee:** Maid Marian, frequently represented as the companion of Robin Hood, was also a character in the Morris dances and May games, which were not notable for their observance of the proprieties. The wife of the deputy of the ward would be a highly respectable woman.

120. **on:** for.

131. **where to have her:** i.e., whether she is fish, allowable every day, or flesh, not permitted on fast days. A second meaning is that her talk skips about so that a man can't keep up with her position.

Prince. What didst thou lose, Jack?

Fal. Wilt thou believe me, Hal, three or four bonds of forty pound apiece and a seal-ring of my grand- 105 father's.

Prince. A trifle, some eightpenny matter.

Hos. So I told him, my lord, and I said I heard your Grace say so; and, my lord, he speaks most vilely of you, like a foulmouthed man as he is, and 110 said he would cudgel you.

Prince. What! he did not?

Hos. There's neither faith, truth, nor womanhood in me else.

Fal. There's no more faith in thee than in a stewed 115 prune, nor no more truth in thee than in a drawn fox; and for womanhood, Maid Marian may be the deputy's wife of the ward to thee. Go, you thing, go!

Hos. Say, what thing? what thing?

Fal. What thing? Why, a thing to thank God on.   120

Hos. I am no thing to thank God on, I would thou shouldst know it! I am an honest man's wife, and, setting thy knighthood aside, thou art a knave to call me so.

Fal. Setting thy womanhood aside, thou art a beast 125 to say otherwise.

Hos. Say, what beast, thou knave, thou?

Fal. What beast? Why, an otter.

Prince. An otter, Sir John? Why an otter?

Fal. Why, she's neither fish nor flesh; a man knows 130 not where to have her.

Hos. Thou art an unjust man in saying so. Thou or any man knows where to have me, thou knave, thou!

137. **ought:** owed; the obsolete past tense of the verb "owe."

154. **I pray God my girdle break:** a reference to the proverb, "Ungirt, unblessed." The girdle was the belt from which a man's sword was suspended.

160. **embossed rascal:** in hunting terminology an **embossed rascal** would be a lean deer driven into a thicket or exhausted; see II. iv. 353. **Embossed** also means swollen or bulging (elaborately decorated with a bulging relief) and the Prince may also intend, by extension, a meaning like extraordinary or egregious.

164. **injuries:** painful losses; that is, objects whose loss would be painful.

Prince. Thou sayst true, hostess, and he slanders
thee most grossly.   135

Hos. So he doth you, my lord, and said this other
day you ought him a thousand pound.

Prince. Sirrah, do I owe you a thousand pound?

Fal. A thousand pound, Hal? A million! Thy love
is worth a million; thou owest me thy love.   140

Hos. Nay, my lord, he called you Jack and said
he would cudgel you.

Fal. Did I, Bardolph?

Bar. Indeed, Sir John, you said so.

Fal. Yea, if he said my ring was copper.   145

Prince. I say 'tis copper. Darest thou be as good as
thy word now?

Fal. Why, Hal, thou knowest, as thou art but man,
I dare; but as thou art Prince, I fear thee as I fear
the roaring of the lion's whelp.   150

Prince. And why not as the lion?

Fal. The King himself is to be feared as the lion.
Dost thou think I'll fear thee as I fear thy father?
Nay, an I do, I pray God my girdle break.

Prince. O, if it should, how would thy guts fall   155
about thy knees! But, sirrah, there's no room for faith,
truth, nor honesty in this bosom of thine. It is all
filled up with guts and midriff. Charge an honest
woman with picking thy pocket? Why, thou whoreson, impudent, embossed rascal, if there were   160
anything in thy pocket but tavern reckonings, mem-
orandums of bawdy houses, and one poor pennyworth of sugar candy to make thee long-winded—if
thy pocket were enriched with any other injuries

165. **stand to it:** stick to your story.

166. **pocket up wrong:** endure insult.

177. **still:** ever; see I. iii. 294.

180. **answered:** taken care of; settled.

188. **with unwashed hands:** i.e., without ceremony.

Falstaff and Mistress Quickly.
From the frontispiece of Francis Kirkman, *The Wits; or, Sport upon Sport* (1672).

but these, I am a villain. And yet you will stand to it; 165
you will not pocket up wrong. Art thou not ashamed?

Fal. Dost thou hear, Hal? Thou knowest in the
state of innocency Adam fell, and what should poor
Jack Falstaff do in the days of villainy? Thou seest I
have more flesh than another man, and therefore 170
more frailty. You confess then, you picked my
pocket?

Prince. It appears so by the story.

Fal. Hostess, I forgive thee. Go make ready breakfast. Love thy husband, look to thy servants, cherish 175
thy guests. Thou shalt find me tractable to any honest
reason. Thou seest I am pacified still. Nay, prithee be
gone.

Exit Hostess.

Now, Hal, to the news at court. For the robbery,
lad—how is that answered? 180

Prince. O my sweet beef, I must still be good angel
to thee. The money is paid back again.

Fal. O, I do not like that paying back! 'Tis a
double labor.

Prince. I am good friends with my father, and may 185
do anything.

Fal. Rob me the exchequer the first thing thou
doest, and do it with unwashed hands too.

Bar. Do, my lord.

Prince. I have procured thee, Jack, a charge of 190
foot.

Fal. I would it had been of horse. Where shall I
find one that can steal well? O for a fine thief of the
age of two-and-twenty or thereabouts! I am hei-

209. **their furniture:** equipment for his charge (company).

212. **brave:** splendid; see I. ii. 65.

nously unprovided. Well, God be thanked for these 195
rebels. They offend none but the virtuous. I laud
them, I praise them.

  Prince. Bardolph!

  Bar. My lord?

  Prince. Go bear this letter to Lord John of 200
    Lancaster,
To my brother John; this to my Lord of Westmore-
    land.   [*Exit Bardolph.*]
Go, Peto, to horse, to horse; for thou and I
Have thirty miles to ride yet ere dinnertime.   205
                                       [*Exit Peto.*]
Jack, meet me tomorrow in the Temple Hall
At two o'clock in the afternoon.
There shalt thou know thy charge, and there receive
Money and order for their furniture.
The land is burning; Percy stands on high;   210
And either they or we must lower lie.   [*Exit.*]

  Fal. Rare words! brave world! Hostess, my break-
    fast, come!
O, I could wish this tavern were my drum!

                                          Exit.

THE HISTORY OF
HENRY
THE FOURTH
[PART 1]

ACT IV

IV. i. Hotspur and Worcester, in their camp, learn that Northumberland is ill and cannot join them immediately. They console themselves for the loss and decide that it will make little difference to their cause, though they receive news that the King, Westmoreland, Prince John, and Prince Hal are all marching to meet them, and that Glendower cannot assemble his forces for another two weeks. Hotspur, Worcester, and Douglas must meet the King and his troops without their own full strength, but Hotspur remains cheerful and undismayed.

⸱⸱⸱⸱⸱⸱⸱⸱⸱⸱⸱⸱⸱⸱⸱⸱⸱⸱⸱⸱⸱⸱⸱⸱⸱⸱⸱⸱⸱⸱⸱⸱

3. **attribution:** credit; reputation.

4. **stamp:** minting.

5. **go so general current:** be so generally valued; see II. iii. 99.

6. **defy:** disdain.

7. **soothers:** flatterers; **braver:** finer; more supreme.

9. **task me to my word:** put my word to the test; **approve:** prove by trial; see I. i. 55.

11-2. **No man so potent . . . But I will beard him:** that is, I will defy any man no matter how powerful.

ACT IV

Scene I. [The rebel camp near Shrewsbury.]

Enter *Hotspur, Worcester,* and *Douglas.*

Hot. Well said, my noble Scot. If speaking truth
In this fine age were not thought flattery,
Such attribution should the Douglas have
As not a soldier of this season's stamp
Should go so general current through the world.   5
By God, I cannot flatter; I do defy
The tongues of soothers; but a braver place
In my heart's love hath no man than yourself.
Nay, task me to my word; approve me, lord.
    Doug. Thou art the king of honor.   10
No man so potent breathes upon the ground
But I will beard him.

Enter *One* with letters.

Hot.   Do so, and 'tis well.—
What letters hast thou there?—I can but thank you.
    Mess. These letters come from your father.   15
    Hot. Letters from him? Why comes he not himself?
    Mess. He cannot come, my lord; he is grievous sick.
    Hot. Zounds! how has he the leisure to be sick

81

19. **justling:** jostling; belligerent; **power:** army.

20. **government:** command.

25. **feared:** feared for.

26. **state of time:** condition of these times; **whole:** sound.

28. **better worth:** more valuable.

34-5. **by deputation could not/So soon be drawn:** could not be gathered together so quickly by anyone acting for himself; **meet:** suitable; advisable.

36. **dear:** important; see I. i. 33.

37. **any soul removed:** any soul outside his own; anyone else.

38. **advertisement:** instruction; admonition.

39. **conjunction:** combination (of troops); **on:** go on; proceed.

42. **possessed:** informed.

46. **His present want:** our present lack of him.

47. **Were it good:** would it be good.

48-9. **set the exact wealth of all our states/ All at one cast:** to risk all our assets on one throw, as in a dice game; **main:** stake; a term from the dice game "hazard."

In such a justling time? Who leads his power?
Under whose government come they along?   20
   Mess. His letters bears his mind, not I, my lord.
   Wor. I prithee tell me, doth he keep his bed?
   Mess. He did, my lord, four days ere I set forth,
And at the time of my departure thence
He was much feared by his physicians.   25
   Wor. I would the state of time had first been whole
Ere he by sickness had been visited.
His health was never better worth than now.
   Hot. Sick now? droop now? This sickness doth in-
     fect   30
The very lifeblood of our enterprise.
'Tis catching hither, even to our camp.
He writes me here that inward sickness—
And that his friends by deputation could not
So soon be drawn; nor did he think it meet   35
To lay so dangerous and dear a trust
On any soul removed but on his own.
Yet doth he give us bold advertisement,
That with our small conjunction we should on,
To see how fortune is disposed to us;   40
For, as he writes, there is no quailing now,
Because the King is certainly possessed
Of all our purposes. What say you to it?
   Wor. Your father's sickness is a maim to us.
   Hot. A perilous gash, a very limb lopped off.   45
And yet, in faith, it is not! His present want
Seems more than we shall find it. Were it good
To set the exact wealth of all our states
All at one cast? to set so rich a main

50. **nice:** dubious.

51. **read:** discover.

53. **list:** limit.

56. **reversion:** promise of good fortune to come. The word is a legal term meaning the right of succession to an office or inheritance of property.

59. **comfort of retirement:** comforting hope of withdrawal.

61-2. **If that:** if; **look big/Upon:** tower over; i.e., menace; **maidenhead:** first stage.

64. **hair:** character; essence.

65. **Brooks:** allows.

67. **mere:** absolute.

69. **apprehension:** conception.

70. **fearful faction:** timid conspiracy; i.e., such conspirators as were half-hearted to begin with.

71. **question in:** doubt of.

72. **off'ring side:** aggressive party.

73. **arbitrament:** assessment and consequent judgment.

79. **strain:** stretch; i.e., you are making too much out of the facts.

On the nice hazard of one doubtful hour?   50
It were not good; for therein should we read
The very bottom and the soul of hope,
The very list, the very utmost bound
Of all our fortunes.

    Doug.   Faith, and so we should;   55
Where now remains a sweet reversion.
We may boldly spend upon the hope
Of what is to come in.
A comfort of retirement lives in this.

    Hot. A rendezvous, a home to fly unto,   60
If that the Devil and mischance look big
Upon the maidenhead of our affairs.

    Wor. But yet I would your father had been here.
The quality and hair of our attempt
Brooks no division. It will be thought   65
By some that know not why he is away,
That wisdom, loyalty, and mere dislike
Of our proceedings kept the Earl from hence.
And think how such an apprehension
May turn the tide of fearful faction   70
And breed a kind of question in our cause.
For well you know we of the off'ring side
Must keep aloof from strict arbitrament,
And stop all sight-holes, every loop from whence
The eye of reason may pry in upon us.   75
This absence of your father's draws a curtain
That shows the ignorant a kind of fear
Before not dreamt of.

    Hot.   You strain too far.
I rather of his absence make this use: 80

82. **dare:** daring.

87. **Yet:** as yet.

102. **daffed:** thrust.

103. **bid it pass:** dismissed it lightly. The phrase was a common one to express unconcern for the serious side of life.

105-6. **estridges:** ostriches; **plumed like estridges that with the wind/Bated, like eagles having lately bathed:** plumed with ostrich feathers that fluttered in the wind as eagles flutter their wings after bathing.

It lends a luster and more great opinion,
A larger dare to our great enterprise,
Than if the Earl were here; for men must think,
If we, without his help, can make a head
To push against a kingdom, with his help   85
We shall o'erturn it topsy-turvy down.
Yet all goes well; yet all our joints are whole.
    Doug. As heart can think. There is not such a
        word
Spoke of in Scotland as this term of fear.   90

            Enter *Sir Richard Vernon.*

    Hot. My cousin Vernon! welcome, by my soul.
    Ver. Pray God my news be worth a welcome, lord.
The Earl of Westmoreland, seven thousand strong,
Is marching hitherwards; with him Prince John.
    Hot. No harm. What more?   95
    Ver.   And further, I have learned
The King himself in person is set forth,
Or hitherwards intended speedily,
With strong and mighty preparation.
    Hot. He shall be welcome too. Where is his son,   100
The nimble-footed madcap Prince of Wales,
And his comrades, that daffed the world aside
And bid it pass?
    Ver.   All furnished, all in arms;
All plumed like estridges that with the wind   105
Bated, like eagles having lately bathed;
Glittering in golden coats like images;
As full of spirit as the month of May
And gorgeous as the sun at midsummer;

110. **Wanton:** frisky.

111. **beaver:** helmet.

112. **cushes:** cuisses; armored thigh pieces.

113. **feathered Mercury:** Mercury, the messenger of the gods, was pictured with winged heels and wings on his helmet, indicating his swiftness.

116. **turn and wind:** i.e., put through his paces in making him wheel about; **Pegasus:** a mythological winged horse.

117. **witch:** enchant.

120. **agues:** a common belief of the time was that the sun caused fevers by drawing infection from the marshes, in spring generally and especially in March.

121. **in their trim:** trimmed (decorated) in their best.

122. **the fire-eyed maid of smoky war:** Bellona, Roman goddess of war.

124. **mailed:** armored; **Mars:** the Roman god of war.

126. **reprisal:** prize.

138. **battle:** army.

Wanton as youthful goats, wild as young bulls.   110
I saw young Harry with his beaver on,
His cushes on his thighs, gallantly armed,
Rise from the ground like feathered Mercury,
And vaulted with such ease into his seat
As if an angel dropped down from the clouds   115
To turn and wind a fiery Pegasus
And witch the world with noble horsemanship.
    Hot. No more, no more! Worse than the sun in
        March,
This praise doth nourish agues. Let them come.   120
They come like sacrifices in their trim,
And to the fire-eyed maid of smoky war
All hot and bleeding will we offer them.
The mailed Mars shall on his altar sit
Up to the ears in blood. I am on fire   125
To hear this rich reprisal is so nigh,
And yet not ours. Come, let me taste my horse,
Who is to bear me like a thunderbolt
Against the bosom of the Prince of Wales.
Harry to Harry shall, hot horse to horse,   130
Meet, and ne'er part till one drop down a corse.
O that Glendower were come!
    Ver.   There is more news.
I learned in Worcester, as I rode along,
He cannot draw his power this fourteen days.   135
    Doug. That's the worst tidings that I hear of yet.
    Wor. Ay, by my faith, that bears a frosty sound.
    Hot. What may the King's whole battle reach
        unto?
    Ver. To thirty thousand.   140

144. **take a muster:** assess our numbers.

146. **am out of fear:** have no fear.

‖‖‖‖‖‖‖‖‖‖‖‖‖‖‖‖‖‖‖‖‖‖‖‖‖‖‖‖‖‖‖‖‖‖‖‖‖

IV. ii. Falstaff, having let all the sound and able-bodied men whom he had impressed buy themselves off, now approaches Coventry with a sorry lot of tatterdemalions. The Prince deplores the quality of Falstaff's men but urges him to hurry to the rendezvous.

‖‖‖‖‖‖‖‖‖‖‖‖‖‖‖‖‖‖‖‖‖‖‖‖‖‖‖‖‖‖

3. **Sutton Co'fil':** Sutton Coldfield, near Birmingham.

5. **Lay out:** lay out the money yourself.

6. **This bottle makes an angel:** i.e., if I pay for this bottle it will make an angel that you owe me. An **angel** was a coin.

7. **An if it do, take it:** Falstaff jests that if the bottle "makes" an angel, Bardolph may keep the angel so made.

8. **answer the coinage:** take responsibility for the counterfeit. Coining was a treasonable offense.

12. **soused gurnet:** pickled gurnard (a small fish); **press:** impressment of soldiers.

16-8. **asked twice on the banes:** i.e., whose marriage banns had twice been read in church. Readings on three consecutive Sundays were necessary before the church wedding; **commodity:** lot; see I. ii. 85; **warm slaves:** well-to-do rascals.

Hot.   Forty let it be.
My father and Glendower being both away,
The powers of us may serve so great a day.
Come, let us take a muster speedily.
Doomsday is near. Die all, die merrily.   145

   Doug. Talk not of dying. I am out of fear
Of death or death's hand for this one half-year.
                        [Exeunt.]

Scene II. [A public road near Coventry.]

Enter Falstaff and Bardolph.

   Fal. Bardolph, get thee before to Coventry; fill me
a bottle of sack. Our soldiers shall march through.
We'll to Sutton Co'fil' tonight.

   Bar. Will you give me money, Captain?

   Fal. Lay out, lay out.   5

   Bar. This bottle makes an angel.

   Fal. An if it do, take it for thy labor; an if it make
twenty, take them all; I'll answer the coinage. Bid
my lieutenant Peto meet me at town's end.

   Bar. I will, Captain. Farewell.   *Exit.*   10

   Fal. If I be not ashamed of my soldiers, I am a
soused gurnet. I have misused the King's press dam-
nably. I have got, in exchange of a hundred and fifty
soldiers, three hundred and odd pounds. I press me
none but good householders, yeomen's sons; inquire   15
me out contracted bachelors, such as had been asked
twice on the banes—such a commodity of warm

19. **caliver:** musket.

21. **toasts-and-butter:** i.e., milksops.

22-3. **bought out their services:** paid Falstaff to let them go.

24-6. **ancients:** ensigns; standard-bearers; **gentlemen of companies:** soldiers of a somewhat higher rating than ordinary enlisted men; **Lazarus in the painted cloth:** wall hangings painted with scenes were modest substitutes for tapestry hangings. Biblical subjects such as Lazarus were popular themes for these decorations.

27-8. **unjust:** dishonest; **younger sons to younger brothers:** the English law of primogeniture gave the right of inheritance to the oldest male. The younger son of a younger brother would therefore be doubly impoverished. Usually the younger brothers learned a trade or profession while the eldest inherited the title and estates if any.

29. **revolted:** runaway; **trade-fall'n:** unemployed; **cankers:** cankerworms; i.e., destructive parasites.

30-1. **more dishonorable ragged:** that is, their raggedness is to their discredit, whereas the **ancient** has become honorably ragged through years of service; **feazed ancient:** tattered flag.

35. **draff:** refuse.

41. **gyves:** fetters.

43. **napkins:** handkerchiefs.

45. **a herald's coat:** a tabard, the sleeveless tunic worn by heralds.

48. **on every hedge:** that is, where housewives had spread it to dry.

slaves as had as lieve hear the Devil as a drum, such
as fear the report of a caliver worse than a struck
fowl or a hurt wild duck. I pressed me none but   20
such toasts-and-butter, with hearts in their bellies no
bigger than pins' heads, and they have bought out
their services; and now my whole charge consists of
ancients, corporals, lieutenants, gentlemen of companies—slaves as ragged as Lazarus in the painted   25
cloth, where the glutton's dogs licked his sores; and
such as indeed were never soldiers, but discarded unjust servingmen, younger sons to younger brothers,
revolted tapsters, and ostlers trade-fall'n; the cankers
of a calm world and a long peace; ten times more dis- 30
honorable ragged than an old feazed ancient; and
such have I to fill up the rooms of them that have
bought out their services that you would think that
I had a hundred and fifty tattered prodigals lately
come from swine-keeping, from eating draff and   35
husks. A mad fellow met me on the way, and told
me I had unloaded all the gibbets and pressed the
dead bodies. No eye hath seen such scarecrows. I'll
not march through Coventry with them, that's flat.
Nay, and the villains march wide betwixt the legs,   40
as if they had gyves on, for indeed I had the most
of them out of prison. There's but a shirt and a half
in all my company, and the half-shirt is two napkins
tacked together and thrown over the shoulders like
a herald's coat without sleeves; and the shirt, to say 45
the truth, stol'n from my host at Saint Alban's, or the
red-nose innkeeper of Daventry. But that's all one;
they'll find linen enough on every hedge.

49. **blown . . . quilt:** swollen . . . padded fellow. More insulting references to Falstaff's girth.

52. **cry you mercy:** beg your pardon. Falstaff has belatedly noticed Westmoreland's presence.

57. **away all night:** spend the night traveling.

60-1. **to steal cream indeed, for thy theft hath already made thee butter:** a pun on steal (stale) cream.

65. **toss:** that is, impale on pikes.

73-4. **three fingers:** flesh to the thickness of three fingers (one and a quarter inches).

Enter the Prince and the Lord of Westmoreland.

Prince. How now, blown Jack? How now, quilt?

Fal. What, Hal? How now, mad wag? What a 50
devil dost thou in Warwickshire? My good Lord of
Westmoreland, I cry you mercy. I thought your
honor had already been at Shrewsbury.

West. Faith, Sir John, 'tis more than time that I
were there, and you too, but my powers are there al- 55
ready. The King, I can tell you, looks for us all. We
must away all night.

Fal. Tut, never fear me: I am as vigilant as a cat
to steal cream.

Prince. I think, to steal cream indeed, for thy theft 60
hath already made thee butter. But tell me, Jack,
whose fellows are these that come after?

Fal. Mine, Hal, mine.

Prince. I did never see such pitiful rascals.

Fal. Tut, tut! good enough to toss; food for pow- 65
der, food for powder. They'll fill a pit as well as
better. Tush, man, mortal men, mortal men.

West. Ay, but, Sir John, methinks they are exceed-
ing poor and bare—too beggarly.

Fal. Faith, for their poverty, I know not where 70
they had that, and for their bareness, I am sure they
never learned that of me.

Prince. No, I'll be sworn, unless you call three
fingers on the ribs bare. But, sirrah, make haste.
Percy is already in the field.   *Exit.* 75

Fal. What, is the King encamped?

West. He is, Sir John. I fear we shall stay too long.

79-81. **To the latter end of a fray and the beginning of a feast/Fits a dull fighter and a keen guest:** proverbial: better come at the latter end of a feast than the beginning of a fray.

||||||||||||||||||||||||||||||||||||||||||||||||||||||

IV. iii. Hotspur and his allies disagree about an immediate night attack. Hotspur and Douglas are eager for battle but Worcester and Vernon think it ill advised. With the matter still undecided, Sir Walter Blunt comes from the King to ask about their grievances. Hotspur declares that the King had originally sought the help of the Percies to regain his inheritance as Duke of Lancaster. Then, having secured the dukedom, he curried favor with the multitude by denouncing King Richard's abuses and finally deposed and killed Richard, the true King. Furthermore, King Henry's taxes are as heavy as Richard's and now, to add to his faults, he allows Mortimer to be held prisoner by the Welsh and makes no effort to pay his ransom. Hotspur suggests that the King's party leave a hostage and the Percies will answer his message in the morning.

||||||||||||||||||||||||||||||||||||||||||||

5. **supply:** reinforcements.

8. **be advised:** take advice.

14. **well-respected honor:** sound considerations of honor; that is, if close examination of the circumstances should indicate that honor requires my action.

15. **hold as little counsel with:** give as little ear to.

Fal. Well,
To the latter end of a fray and the beginning of a
   feast   80
Fits a dull fighter and a keen guest.

                                            Exeunt.

Scene III. [The rebel camp near Shrewsbury.]

Enter *Hotspur, Worcester, Douglas, Vernon.*

Hot. We'll fight with him tonight.
Wor.   It may not be.
Doug. You give him then advantage.
Ver.   Not a whit.
Hot. Why say you so? Looks he not for supply?   5
Ver. So do we.
Hot.   His is certain, ours is doubtful.
Wor. Good cousin, be advised; stir not tonight.
Ver. Do not, my lord.
Doug.   You do not counsel well.   10
You speak it out of fear and cold heart.
   Ver. Do me no slander, Douglas. By my life,
And I dare well maintain it with my life,
If well-respected honor bid me on,
I hold as little counsel with weak fear   15
As you, my lord, or any Scot that this day lives.
Let it be seen tomorrow in the battle
Which of us fears.
   Doug.   Yea, or tonight.
   Ver.   Content.   20

23. **of such great leading:** i.e., so accustomed to military command.

25. **expedition:** speed; **horse:** cavalry.

28. **pride:** spirit.

32. **journey-bated:** abated (weakened) by travel; see **bate,** III. iii. 2.

S.D. after l. 35. **parley:** a distinctive trumpet call as an order to hold fire.

37. **respect:** consideration in the sense of "thoughtful attention"; see **respected** at l. 14.

40. **determination:** conviction.

43. **quality:** party.

45. **defend:** forbid.

46. **out of limit and true rule:** beyond the limits of order and rightful government.

48. **charge:** duty—the message I bear.

Hot. Tonight, say I.

Ver. Come, come, it may not be. I wonder much,
Being men of such great leading as you are,
That you foresee not what impediments
Drag back our expedition. Certain horse   25
Of my cousin Vernon's are not yet come up.
Your uncle Worcester's horse came but today;
And now their pride and mettle is asleep,
Their courage with hard labor tame and dull,
That not a horse is half the half of himself.   30

Hot. So are the horses of the enemy
In general journey-bated and brought low.
The better part of ours are full of rest.

Wor. The number of the King exceedeth ours.
For God's sake, cousin, stay till all come in.   35
                    The trumpet sounds a parley.

Enter *Sir Walter Blunt.*

Blunt. I come with gracious offers from the King,
If you vouchsafe me hearing and respect.

Hot. Welcome, Sir Walter Blunt, and would to
    God
You were of our determination.   40
Some of us love you well; and even those some
Envy your great deservings and good name,
Because you are not of our quality,
But stand against us like an enemy.

Blunt. And God defend but still I should stand so,   45
So long as out of limit and true rule
You stand against anointed majesty.
But to my charge. The King hath sent to know

49. **griefs:** grievances.

50. **conjure:** bring out, as though by enchantment; **civil:** gentle.

58. **suggestion:** evil prompting.

63. **not six-and-twenty strong:** supported by fewer than twenty-six followers.

69. **sue his livery:** sue for the restoration of the property due him by inheritance from his father.

70. **terms of zeal:** expressions of ardent loyalty.

75. **more and less:** great and small; **with cap and knee:** that is, offering homage.

The nature of your griefs, and whereupon
You conjure from the breast of civil peace   50
Such bold hostility, teaching his duteous land
Audacious cruelty. If that the King
Have any way your good deserts forgot,
Which he confesseth to be manifold,
He bids you name your griefs, and with all speed   55
You shall have your desires with interest,
And pardon absolute for yourself and these
Herein misled by your suggestion.

   Hot. The King is kind, and well we know the King
Knows at what time to promise, when to pay.   60
My father and my uncle and myself
Did give him that same royalty he wears;
And when he was not six-and-twenty strong,
Sick in the world's regard, wretched and low,
A poor unminded outlaw sneaking home,   65
My father gave him welcome to the shore;
And when he heard him swear and vow to God
He came but to be Duke of Lancaster,
To sue his livery and beg his peace,
With tears of innocency and terms of zeal,   70
My father, in kind heart and pity moved,
Swore him assistance, and performed it too.
Now when the lords and barons of the the realm
Perceived Northumberland did lean to him,
The more and less came in with cap and knee;   75
Met him in boroughs, cities, villages,
Attended him on bridges, stood in lanes,
Laid gifts before him, proffered him their oaths,
Gave him their heirs as pages, followed him

81. **as greatness knows itself:** as he realizes his own power.

85. **forsooth:** in truth; see I. iii. 147.

86. **strait:** strict.

88. **Cries out upon:** declaims against.

89-90. **this face,/This seeming brow:** this disguise, this semblance.

95. **personal:** that is, personally occupied.

100. **in the neck of:** on top of; **tasked:** taxed; that is, literally laid a tax on. One of King Henry's criticisms of Richard II was that he taxed the people too heavily. The Percies, when disgruntled with the King, accused him of a similar fault.

102. **if every owner were well placed:** if everyone had his rights.

103. **engaged:** pledged as a hostage.

105. **Disgraced me in my happy victories:** a reference to the King's demand for the captives taken by the Percies. **Happy** means fortunate.

106. **intelligence:** espionage.

107. **Rated:** drove away abusively.

Even at the heels in golden multitudes.   80
He presently, as greatness knows itself,
Steps me a little higher than his vow
Made to my father, while his blood was poor,
Upon the naked shore at Ravenspurgh;
And now, forsooth, takes on him to reform   85
Some certain edicts and some strait decrees
That lie too heavy on the commonwealth;
Cries out upon abuses, seems to weep
Over his country's wrongs; and by this face,
This seeming brow of justice, did he win   90
The hearts of all that he did angle for;
Proceeded further—cut me off the heads
Of all the favorites that the absent King
In deputation left behind him here
When he was personal in the Irish war.   95
    Blunt. Tut! I came not to hear this.
    Hot. Then to the point.
In short time after, he deposed the King;
Soon after that deprived him of his life;
And in the neck of that tasked the whole state;   100
To make that worse, suff'red his kinsman March
(Who is, if every owner were well placed,
Indeed his king) to be engaged in Wales,
There without ransom to lie forfeited;
Disgraced me in my happy victories,   105
Sought to entrap me by intelligence;
Rated mine uncle from the council board;
In rage dismissed my father from the court;
Broke oath on oath, committed wrong on wrong;
And in conclusion drove us to seek out   110

111. **head of safety:** army to protect us.

113. **indirect:** irregular; not as sound as it might be.

116. **impawned:** pledged.

120. **grace:** forgiveness.

<hr>

IV. iv. The Archbishop of York, a party to the Percy conspiracy, is fearful of the outcome and sends messages to his friends. If Percy and his allies are defeated, he himself must expect the King's punishment.

<hr>

1. **Hie:** hurry; **brief:** dispatch.

2. **lord marshal:** Thomas Mowbray, son of that Duke of Norfolk whose quarrel with Bolingbroke had occasioned their exile by Richard II.

10. **bide the touch:** endure the test.

This head of safety, and withal to pry
Into his title, the which we find
Too indirect for long continuance.

   Blunt. Shall I return this answer to the King?

   Hot. Not so, Sir Walter. We'll withdraw awhile. 115
Go to the King; and let there be impawned
Some surety for a safe return again,
And in the morning early shall mine uncle
Bring him our purposes; and so farewell.

   Blunt. I would you would accept of grace and love. 120

   Hot. And may be so we shall.

   Blunt.   Pray God you do.

                                  Exeunt.

Scene IV. [York. The Archbishop's palace.]

Enter the Archbishop of York and Sir Michael.

   Arch. Hie, good Sir Michael; bear this sealed brief
With winged haste to the lord marshal;
This to my cousin Scroop; and all the rest
To whom they are directed. If you knew
How much they do import, you would make haste.   5

   Sir M. My good lord, I guess their tenor.

   Arch. Like enough you do.
Tomorrow, good Sir Michael, is a day
Wherein the fortune of ten thousand men
Must bide the touch; for, sir, at Shrewsbury,   10
As I am truly given to understand,
The King with mighty and quick-raised power
Meets with Lord Harry; and I fear, Sir Michael,

15. Whose power was in the first proportion: who commanded the greatest military power.

17. a rated sinew: valued as a chief supporting force.

18. overruled: swayed; governed.

32-3. mo: more; **corrivals:** associates; see I. iii. 217; **dear men/Of estimation and command in arms:** valuable men, whose experience in military command is highly regarded.

Soldiers marching to fife and drum.
From a seventeenth-century ballad.

What with the sickness of Northumberland,
Whose power was in the first proportion,   15
And what with Owen Glendower's absence thence,
Who with them was a rated sinew too
And comes not in, overruled by prophecies—
I fear the power of Percy is too weak
To wage an instant trial with the King.   20
　　Sir M. Why, my good lord, you need not fear;
There is Douglas and Lord Mortimer.
　　Arch. No, Mortimer is not there.
　　Sir M. But there is Mordake, Vernon, Lord Harry
　　　　Percy,   25
And there is my Lord of Worcester, and a head
Of gallant warriors, noble gentlemen.
　　Arch. And so there is; but yet the King hath drawn
The special head of all the land together—
The Prince of Wales, Lord John of Lancaster,   30
The noble Westmoreland and warlike Blunt,
And many mo corrivals and dear men
Of estimation and command in arms.
　　Sir M. Doubt not, my lord, they shall be well op-
　　　　posed.   35
　　Arch. I hope no less, yet needful 'tis to fear;
And, to prevent the worst, Sir Michael, speed.
For if Lord Percy thrive not, ere the King
Dismiss his power, he means to visit us,
For he hath heard of our confederacy,   40
And 'tis but wisdom to make strong against him.
Therefore make haste. I must go write again
To other friends; and so farewell, Sir Michael.
　　　　　　　　　　　　　　　　　Exeunt.

THE HISTORY OF
HENRY
THE FOURTH
[PART 1]

ACT V

V. i. Worcester visits the King's camp to present the Percies' grievances. The King replies and the Prince adds his message and sends a personal challenge to Hotspur, whom he praises for his valor. The King promises full pardon to the rebels if they will come to terms now, but neither he nor the Prince believe that Hotspur and Douglas will agree to a peaceful settlement.

Falstaff is apprehensive of the coming battle and philosophizes about honor, which he concludes is air, nothing but a word, and he will have none of it.

▬▬▬▬▬▬▬▬▬▬▬▬▬

2. **busky:** bosky; wooded.

3. **his:** its; the sun's; **distemp'rature:** extraordinary appearance.

5. **Doth play the trumpet to his purposes:** i.e., acts as a herald to what the sun's appearance threatens.

8. **sympathize:** harmonize.

ACT V

Scene I. [The King's camp near Shrewsbury.]

Enter the King, Prince of Wales, Lord John of Lancaster, Sir Walter Blunt, Falstaff.

King. How bloodily the sun begins to peer
Above yon busky hill! The day looks pale
At his distemp'rature.
   Prince.   The southern wind
Doth play the trumpet to his purposes   5
And by his hollow whistling in the leaves
Foretells a tempest and a blust'ring day.
   King. Then with the losers let it sympathize,
For nothing can seem foul to those that win.

The trumpet sounds. Enter *Worcester* [and *Vernon*].

How now, my Lord of Worcester? 'Tis not well   10
That you and I should meet upon such terms
As now we meet. You have deceived our trust
And made us doff our easy robes of peace
To crush our old limbs in ungentle steel.
This is not well, my lord; this is not well.   15

18. **obedient orb:** orbit governed by the laws of nature; i.e., resume your normal course of obedience.

20. **exhaled meteor:** an emanation of gas from one of the heavenly bodies; such manifestations were considered omens of disaster; see I. i. 10-1.

21. **prodigy of fear:** fearful omen.

22. **broached:** broken open; loosed. The figure is from "broaching," i.e., tapping, a keg of liquor.

25. **entertain:** occupy.

27. **dislike:** dissension.

30. **chewet:** chough; a chattering bird.

33. **remember:** remind.

36. **posted:** rode post—the fastest method of travel.

45. **new-fall'n:** newly inherited.

What say you to it? Will you again unknit
This churlish knot of all-abhorred war,
And move in that obedient orb again
Where you did give a fair and natural light,
And be no more an exhaled meteor, 20
A prodigy of fear, and a portent
Of broached mischief to the unborn times?
   Wor. Hear me, my liege.
For mine own part, I could be well content
To entertain the lag-end of my life 25
With quiet hours, for I do protest
I have not sought the day of this dislike.
   King. You have not sought it? How comes it then?
   Fal. Rebellion lay in his way, and he found it.
   Prince. Peace, chewet, peace! 30
   Wor. It pleased your Majesty to turn your looks
Of favor from myself and all our house;
And yet I must remember you, my lord,
We were the first and dearest of your friends.
For you my staff of office did I break 35
In Richard's time, and posted day and night
To meet you on the way and kiss your hand
When yet you were in place and in account
Nothing so strong and fortunate as I.
It was myself, my brother, and his son 40
That brought you home and boldly did outdare
The dangers of the time. You swore to us,
And you did swear that oath at Doncaster,
That you did nothing purpose 'gainst the state,
Nor claim no further than your new-fall'n right, 45
The seat of Gaunt, dukedom of Lancaster.

51. **injuries:** wrongs; **wanton:** undisciplined; unruly.

52. **sufferances:** sufferings.

58. **gripe:** grasp.

61. **gull:** unfledged bird.

64. **our love:** we, your devoted friends.

68. **by such means:** for such reasons.

70. **dangerous countenance:** menacing behavior.

71. **troth:** sworn promise.

73. **articulate:** articulated; specifically itemized.

75. **face:** decorate, and at the same time, conceal the true nature of.

76. **color:** disguise; see I. iii. 112.

To this we swore our aid. But in short space
It rained down fortune show'ring on your head,
And such a flood of greatness fell on you—
What with our help, what with the absent King,   50
What with the injuries of a wanton time,
The seeming sufferances that you had borne,
And the contrarious winds that held the King
So long in his unlucky Irish wars
That all in England did repute him dead—   55
And from this swarm of fair advantages
You took occasion to be quickly wooed
To gripe the general sway into your hand;
Forgot your oath to us at Doncaster;
And, being fed by us, you used us so   60
As that ungentle gull, the cuckoo's bird,
Useth the sparrow—did oppress our nest;
Grew by our feeding to so great a bulk
That even our love durst not come near your sight
For fear of swallowing; but with nimble wing   65
We were enforced for safety sake to fly
Out of your sight and raise this present head;
Whereby we stand opposed by such means
As you yourself have forged against yourself
By unkind usage, dangerous countenance,   70
And violation of all faith and troth
Sworn to us in your younger enterprise.
    King. These things, indeed, you have articulate,
Proclaimed at market crosses, read in churches,
To face the garment of rebellion   75
With some fine color that may please the eye

80. **want:** lack; see IV. i. 46.

81. **water colors:** flimsy excuses.

86. **join in trial:** meet in a contest of arms.

88. **hopes:** that is, hopes of salvation.

89. **set off his head:** not charged against him; that is, if we forgive him his present rebellion.

97. **before my father's Majesty:** i.e., I swear on my father's Majesty.

Of fickle changelings and poor discontents,
Which gape and rub the elbow at the news
Of hurlyburly innovation.
And never yet did insurrection want   80
Such water colors to impaint his cause,
Nor moody beggars, starving for a time
Of pell-mell havoc and confusion.

   Prince. In both our armies there is many a soul
Shall pay full dearly for this encounter,   85
If once they join in trial. Tell your nephew
The Prince of Wales doth join with all the world
In praise of Henry Percy. By my hopes,
This present enterprise set off his head,
I do not think a braver gentleman,   90
More active-valiant or more valiant-young,
More daring or more bold, is now alive
To grace this latter age with noble deeds.
For my part, I may speak it to my shame,
I have a truant been to chivalry;   95
And so I hear he doth account me too.
Yet this before my father's Majesty—
I am content that he shall take the odds
Of his great name and estimation,
And will, to save the blood on either side,   100
Try fortune with him in a single fight.

   King. And, Prince of Wales, so dare we venture
    thee,
Albeit considerations infinite
Do make against it. No, good Worcester, no!   105
We love our people well; even those we love

107. **misled upon your cousin's part:** misled into supporting your kinsman.

113. **wait on us:** serve me.

114. **do their office:** perform their duty.

116. **take it advisedly:** be advised and take our offer.

124. **bestride me:** i.e., stand over me and fight in my defense; **so:** good.

125. **colossus:** a man of monstrous size. The word comes from the Colossus of Rhodes, a gigantic statue of the sun god that stood near the harbor of Rhodes and was accounted one of the Seven Wonders of the classical world. It was destroyed in the third century B.C., but Elizabethans pictured it as guarding the harbor, as the illustration shows.

132. **prick me off:** that is, select me for death.

133. **set to:** heal or make whole again.

An artist's conception of the Colossus of Rhodes.
From André Thevet, *Cosmographie de Levant* (1554).

That are misled upon your cousin's part;
And, will they take the offer of our grace,
Both he, and they, and you, yea, every man
Shall be my friend again, and I'll be his.   110
So tell your cousin, and bring me word
What he will do. But if he will not yield,
Rebuke and dread correction wait on us,
And they shall do their office. So be gone.
We will not now be troubled with reply.   115
We offer fair; take it advisedly.

              Exit Worcester [with Vernon].

  Prince. It will not be accepted, on my life.
The Douglas and the Hotspur both together
Are confident against the world in arms.

  King. Hence, therefore, every leader to his charge; 120
For, on their answer, will we set on them,
And God befriend us as our cause is just!

            Exeunt. Manent Prince, Falstaff.

  Fal. Hal, if thou see me down in the battle and
bestride me, so! 'Tis a point of friendship.

  Prince. Nothing but a colossus can do thee that 125
friendship. Say thy prayers, and farewell.

  Fal. I would 'twere bedtime, Hal, and all well.

  Prince. Why, thou owest God a death.   *[Exit.]*

  Fal. 'Tis not due yet: I would be loath to pay him
before his day. What need I be so forward with him 130
that calls not on me? Well, 'tis no matter; honor
pricks me on. Yea, but how if honor prick me off
when I come on? How then? Can honor set to a leg?
No. Or an arm? No. Or take away the grief of a

137. **trim:** fine (ironical); **reckoning:** total.

139. **insensible:** not to be discerned by the senses.

141. **Detraction:** slander; **suffer:** permit.

142. **scutcheon:** escutcheon: coat of arms displayed or carried at a funeral; therefore, a glory for the dead.

███████████████████████████████████

V. ii. Worcester reports the King's message to Vernon, but determines to keep Hotspur ignorant of the King's liberality. He tells Hotspur that there is no mercy in the King and delivers the Prince's challenge. All prepare to arm for battle and Hotspur urges everyone to fight valiantly for honor's sake.

███████████████████████████

10. **Supposition . . . shall be stuck full of eyes:** that is, we will always be watched with eyes of suspicion.

14. **or . . . or:** either . . . or.

15. **misquote:** make inaccurate note of.

wound? No. Honor hath no skill in surgery then? No.   135
What is honor? A word. What is in that word honor?
What is that honor? Air—a trim reckoning! Who hath
it? He that died a Wednesday. Doth he feel it? No.
Doth he hear it? No. 'Tis insensible then? Yea, to the
dead. But will it not live with the living? No. Why?   140
Detraction will not suffer it. Therefore I'll none of it.
Honor is a mere scutcheon—and so ends my cate-
chism.

Exit.

Scene II. [The rebel camp near Shrewsbury.]

Enter *Worcester* and *Sir Richard Vernon.*

Wor. O, no, my nephew must not know, Sir
   Richard,
The liberal and kind offer of the King.
  Ver. 'Twere best he did.
  Wor.   Then are we all undone.   5
It is not possible, it cannot be,
The King should keep his word in loving us.
He will suspect us still and find a time
To punish this offense in other faults.
Supposition all our lives shall be stuck full of eyes;   10
For treason is but trusted like the fox,
Who, ne'er so tame, so cherished and locked up,
Will have a wild trick of his ancestors.
Look how we can, or sad or merrily,
Interpretation will misquote our looks,   15

20. **an adopted name of privilege:** i.e., a nickname characterizing him, which makes his action seem the result of his hasty temper.

21. **spleen:** irrational impulse; see II. iii. 83.

22. **live upon my head:** i.e., will remain charged to my account; see V. i. 89.

23. **train:** entice.

25. **spring:** source.

28. **Deliver:** report.

36. **Marry, and shall:** indeed I shall.

40. **mended:** amended; atoned for.

41. **forswearing that he is forsworn:** denying that he has broken his oath.

42. **scourge:** punish.

43. **hateful name:** i.e., of rebels and traitors.

And we shall feed like oxen at a stall,
The better cherished still the nearer death.
My nephew's trespass may be well forgot;
It hath the excuse of youth and heat of blood,
And an adopted name of privilege—   20
A harebrained Hotspur, governed by a spleen.
All his offenses live upon my head
And on his father's. We did train him on;
And, his corruption being ta'en from us,
We, as the spring of all, shall pay for all.   25
Therefore, good cousin, let not Harry know,
In any case, the offer of the King.

                    Enter Hotspur [and Douglas].

    Ver. Deliver what you will, I'll say 'tis so.
Here comes your cousin.
    Hot.   My uncle is returned.   30
Deliver up my Lord of Westmoreland.
Uncle, what news?
    Wor. The King will bid you battle presently.
    Doug. Defy him by the Lord of Westmoreland.
    Hot. Lord Douglas, go you and tell him so.   35
    Doug. Marry, and shall, and very willingly. *Exit.*
    Wor. There is no seeming mercy in the King.
    Hot. Did you beg any? God forbid!
    Wor. I told him gently of our grievances,
Of his oath-breaking, which he mended thus,   40
By now forswearing that he is forsworn.
He calls us rebels, traitors, and will scourge
With haughty arms this hateful name in us.

52. **draw short breath:** pant in battle.

53. **Harry Monmouth:** the Prince was so known because he was born in Monmouth.

54. **tasking:** challenge.

56. **urged:** presented.

59. **gave you all the duties of a man:** gave you full credit for manliness.

63. **dispraising praise valued with you:** denying that any praise was worthy of you.

65. **cital:** recital; account.

68. **instantly:** in the same instant.

70. **envy:** malice; hostility.

71. **owe:** own.

[Re-]enter *Douglas*.

Doug. Arm, gentlemen! to arms! for I have thrown
A brave defiance in King Henry's teeth,   45
And Westmoreland, that was engaged, did bear it;
Which cannot choose but bring him quickly on.

Wor. The Prince of Wales stepped forth before the
    King
And, nephew, challenged you to single fight.   50

Hot. O would the quarrel lay upon our heads,
And that no man might draw short breath today
But I and Harry Monmouth! Tell me, tell me,
How showed his tasking? Seemed it in contempt?

Ver. No, by my soul. I never in my life   55
Did hear a challenge urged more modestly,
Unless a brother should a brother dare
To gentle exercise and proof of arms.
He gave you all the duties of a man;
Trimmed up your praises with a princely tongue;   60
Spoke your deservings like a chronicle;
Making you ever better than his praise
By still dispraising praise valued with you;
And, which became him like a prince indeed,
He made a blushing cital of himself,   65
And chid his truant youth with such a grace
As if he mast'red there a double spirit
Of teaching and of learning instantly.
There did he pause; but let me tell the world,
If he outlive the envy of this day,   70
England did never owe so sweet a hope,

72. **misconstrued in his wantonness:** misunderstood because of his undisciplined wildness; see **wanton,** V. i. 51.

80-2. **Better . . . persuasion:** i.e., you can better stir your own valor by thinking of the deeds you must do than I, who am not eloquent, can stir you by speech.

90. **brave:** splendid; glorious.

So much misconstrued in his wantonness.
  Hot. Cousin, I think thou art enamored
On his follies. Never did I hear
Of any prince so wild a libertine.   75
But be he as he will, yet once ere night
I will embrace him with a soldier's arm,
That he shall shrink under my courtesy.
Arm, arm with speed! and, fellows, soldiers, friends,
Better consider what you have to do   80
Than I, that have not well the gift of tongue,
Can lift your blood up with persuasion.

                Enter a *Messenger.*

  Mess. My lord, here are letters for you.
  Hot. I cannot read them now.—
O gentlemen, the time of life is short!   85
To spend that shortness basely were too long
If life did ride upon a dial's point,
Still ending at the arrival of an hour.
An if we live, we live to tread on kings;
If die, brave death, when princes die with us!   90
Now for our consciences, the arms are fair,
When the intent of bearing them is just.

             Enter another *Messenger.*

  Mess. My lord, prepare. The King comes on apace.
  Hot. I thank him that he cuts me from my tale,
For I profess not talking. Only this—   95
Let each man do his best; and here draw I

99. **adventure:** hazard.

100. **Espérance! Percy:** The Percy rallying cry; see II. iii. 76.

103. **heaven to earth:** the odds are certain.

━━━━━━━━━━━━━━━━━━━━━━━━━━━

V. [iii.] Douglas encounters Sir Walter Blunt attired like the King, and kills him. Falstaff, finding Blunt, again philosophizes about the hollowness of "honor." The Prince comes upon him but leaves in disgust when Falstaff offers him a bottle of sack instead of his pistol. Sir John clings to his preference for life over an honorable death.

━━━━━━━━━━━━━━━━━━━━━━━━━━━

Ent. **Alarum:** trumpet summons.

A sword whose temper I intend to stain
With the best blood that I can meet withal
In the adventure of this perilous day.
Now, Espérance! Percy! and set on.   100
Sound all the lofty instruments of war,
And by that music let us all embrace;
For, heaven to earth, some of us never shall
A second time do such a courtesy.
   Here they embrace. The trumpets sound. [*Exeunt.*]

[Scene III. Another part of the field.]

The King *enters with his Power. Alarum to the battle.*
  [*Exeunt.*] *Then enter* Douglas *and* Sir Walter Blunt.

  Blunt. What is thy name, that in battle thus
Thou crossest me? What honor dost thou seek
Upon my head?
  Doug.   Know then my name is Douglas,
And I do haunt thee in the battle thus   5
Because some tell me that thou art a king.
  Blunt. They tell thee true.
  Doug. The Lord of Stafford dear today hath bought
Thy likeness, for instead of thee, King Harry,
This sword hath ended him. So shall it thee,   10
Unless thou yield thee as my prisoner.
  Blunt. I was not born a yielder, thou proud Scot;
And thou shalt find a king that will revenge
Lord Stafford's death.

24. **Semblably furnished like:** equipped to resemble.

25. **A fool go with thy soul:** that is, the appellation "fool."

28. **in his coats:** that is, wearing the King's insignia. It was common to have decoys of this sort to safeguard the King's life.

33. **stand full fairly:** that is, are in a fair way to win the day.

34. **shot-free:** without paying a tavern reckoning ("shot" or "scot").

35. **scoring:** marking up an account, item by item; an obvious pun.

37. **Here's no vanity:** Falstaff refers to himself and asserts that no such vain desire of honor will possess him.

They fight. Douglas kills Blunt. Then enter Hotspur.

Hot. O Douglas, hadst thou fought at Holmedon   15
   thus,
I never had triumphed upon a Scot.
   Doug. All's done, all's won. Here breathless lies the
   King.
   Hot. Where?   20
   Doug. Here.
   Hot. This, Douglas? No. I know this face full well.
A gallant knight he was, his name was Blunt;
Semblably furnished like the King himself.
   Doug. A fool go with thy soul, whither it goes!   25
A borrowed title hast thou bought too dear:
Why didst thou tell me that thou wert a king?
   Hot. The King hath many marching in his coats.
   Doug. Now, by my sword, I will kill all his coats;
I'll murder all his wardrobe, piece by piece,   30
Until I meet the King.
   Hot.   Up and away!
Our soldiers stand full fairly for the day.   *Exeunt.*

Alarum. Enter *Falstaff solus.*

Fal. Though I could 'scape shot-free at London, I
fear the shot here. Here's no scoring but upon the   35
pate. Soft! who are you? Sir Walter Blunt. There's
honor for you! Here's no vanity! I am as hot as
molten lead, and as heavy too. God keep lead out of
me. I need no more weight than mine own bowels. I

40. peppered: killed; see II. iv. 193.

42. for the town's end, to beg: the edge of town was the resort of beggars.

51. Turk Gregory: perhaps a reference to Pope Gregory XIII, whom many Elizabethans pictured as little better than a barbarous Turk because he had sanctioned the Massacre of St. Bartholomew's Eve and offered an indulgence to anyone who would murder Queen Elizabeth.

52. paid: settled him for good; killed him; see II. iv. 194.

53. sure: safe; that is, we don't have to worry about him any more. The Prince, however, replies that Hotspur is indeed "safe."

64. a carbonado: that is, hacked flesh. A **carbonado** was a piece of meat or fowl slashed crosswise and then grilled.

have led my rag-of-muffins where they are peppered.   40
There's not three of my hundred and fifty left alive,
and they are for the town's end, to beg during life.
But who comes here?

Enter the *Prince*.

Prince. What, standst thou idle here? Lend me thy
    sword.   45
Many a nobleman lies stark and stiff
Under the hoofs of vaunting enemies,
Whose deaths are yet unrevenged. I prithee
Lend me thy sword.

Fal. O Hal, I prithee give me leave to breathe   50
awhile. Turk Gregory never did such deeds in arms
as I have done this day. I have paid Percy; I have
made him sure.

Prince. He is indeed, and living to kill thee.
I prithee lend me thy sword.   55

Fal. Nay, before God, Hal, if Percy be alive, thou
getst not my sword; but take my pistol, if thou wilt.

Prince. Give it me. What, is it in the case?

Fal. Ay, Hal. 'Tis hot, 'tis hot. There's that will
sack a city.   *The Prince draws it out and finds it to*   60
be a bottle of sack.

Prince. What, is it a time to jest and dally now?
    He throws the bottle at him. Exit.

Fal. Well, if Percy be alive, I'll pierce him. If he
do come in my way, so; if he do not, if I come in his
willingly, let him make a carbonado of me. I like not
such grinning honor as Sir Walter hath. Give me life;   65

V. [iv.] The King's forces are in retreat and Hal is wounded. Douglas at last finds the King and is about to kill him until Hal intervenes and forces Douglas to fly for his own life. When Hotspur appears, Hal declares that England is too small for both of them. They fight and Hotspur is killed. In the meantime, Douglas reappears and fights with Falstaff, who feigns death. The Prince sees the prostrate Falstaff and thinks him dead. Falstaff at length revives and seeing Hotspur dead gives him another wound and sets off with the body, planning to claim the honor of having killed him. When Hal comes back with Prince John, he allows Falstaff temporarily to have his glory, and Falstaff follows them off, speculating on the advancement he can expect for such a deed of valor.

||||||||||||||||||||||||||||||||||

Ent. **Excursions:** clashes of arms.
5. **make up:** advance; return to the attack.
6. **amaze:** fill with consternation; terrify.
15. **breathe:** pause; rest.

which if I can save, so; if not, honor comes unlooked
for, and there's an end.

                                                    Exit.

Scene [IV. Another part of the field.]

Alarum. Excursions. Enter the *King*, the *Prince*, *Lord*
    John of Lancaster, *Earl of Westmoreland.*

King. I prithee, Harry, withdraw thyself; thou
    bleedest too much.
Lord John of Lancaster, go you with him.
    John. Not I, my lord, unless I did bleed too.
    Prince. I do beseech your Majesty make up,   5
Lest your retirement do amaze your friends.
    King. I will do so.
My Lord of Westmoreland, lead him to his tent.
    West. Come, my lord, I'll lead you to your tent.
    Prince. Lead me, my lord? I do not need your help;   10
And God forbid a shallow scratch should drive
The Prince of Wales from such a field as this,
Where stained nobility lies trodden on,
And rebels' arms triumph in massacres!
    John. We breathe too long. Come, cousin   15
        Westmoreland,
Our duty this way lies. For God's sake, come.
        [*Exeunt Prince John and Westmoreland.*]
    Prince. By God, thou hast deceived me, Lancaster!
I did not think thee lord of such a spirit.
Before, I loved thee as a brother, John;   20

22. **at the point:** i.e., of his sword.

23. **lustier maintenance:** more vigorous perseverance.

26-7 **Hydra's heads:** the serpent in Greek mythology known as **Hydra** had numerous heads and grew two as soon as one was cut off.

33. **shadows:** counterparts; imitations.

34. **very:** real.

37. **assay:** try (in combat).

42. **like:** likely.

But now, I do respect thee as my soul.
  King. I saw him hold Lord Percy at the point
With lustier maintenance than I did look for
Of such an ungrown warrior.
  Prince. O, this boy lends mettle to us all!   *Exit.* 25

[Enter *Douglas*.]

  Doug. Another King? They grow like Hydra's
        heads.
I am the Douglas, fatal to all those
That wear those colors on them. What art thou
That counterfeitst the person of a king?   30
  King. The King himself, who, Douglas, grieves at
        heart
So many of his shadows thou hast met,
And not the very King. I have two boys
Seek Percy and thyself about the field;   35
But, seeing thou fallst on me so luckily,
I will assay thee. So defend thyself.
  Doug. I fear thou art another counterfeit;
And yet, in faith, thou bearest thee like a king.
But mine I am sure thou art, whoe'er thou be,   40
And thus I win thee.
        They fight, the King being in danger.

Enter *Prince of Wales.*

  Prince. Hold up thy head, vile Scot, or thou art like
Never to hold it up again. The spirits
Of valiant Shirley, Stafford, Blunt are in my arms.

47. **Cheerly:** that is, take heart.
49. **straight:** at once.
51. **opinion:** reputation.
52. **makest some tender of:** place some value on.
55. **heark'ned for:** sought to hear news of; i.e., would welcome.
57. **insulting:** proudly exultant.

It is the Prince of Wales that threatens thee,   45
Who never promiseth but he means to pay.

They fight. Douglas flieth.

Cheerly, my lord. How fares your Grace?
Sir Nicholas Gawsey hath for succor sent,
And so hath Clifton. I'll to Clifton straight.

King. Stay and breathe awhile.   50
Thou hast redeemed thy lost opinion,
And showed thou makest some tender of my life,
In this fair rescue thou hast brought to me.

Prince. O God, they did me too much injury
That ever said I heark'ned for your death.   55
If it were so, I might have let alone
The insulting hand of Douglas over you,
Which would have been as speedy in your end
As all the poisonous potions in the world,
And saved the treacherous labor of your son.   60

King. Make up to Clifton; I'll to Sir Nicholas
   Gawsey.   *Exit.*

Enter *Hotspur.*

Hot. If I mistake not, thou art Harry Monmouth.
Prince. Thou speakst as if I would deny my name.
Hot. My name is Harry Percy.   65
Prince.   Why, then I see
A very valiant rebel of the name.
I am the Prince of Wales, and think not, Percy,
To share with me in glory any more.
Two stars keep not their motion in one sphere,   70
Nor can one England brook a double reign

77. **crest:** helmet.
79. **vanities:** vain boasts.
80. **Well said:** well done.
88. **takes survey of:** superintends.

Of Harry Percy and the Prince of Wales.

   Hot. Nor shall it, Harry, for the hour is come
To end the one of us; and would to God
Thy name in arms were now as great as mine!   75

   Prince. I'll make it greater ere I part from thee,
And all the budding honors on thy crest
I'll crop to make a garland for my head.

   Hot. I can no longer brook thy vanities.

                                  They fight.

Enter *Falstaff.*

   Fal. Well said, Hal! to it, Hal! Nay, you shall find 80
no boy's play here, I can tell you.

   *[Re-]enter Douglas. He fighteth with Falstaff, who
     falls down as if he were dead. [Exit Douglas.]
                  The Prince killeth Percy.*

   Hot. O Harry, thou hast robbed me of my youth!
I better brook the loss of brittle life
Than those proud titles thou hast won of me.
They wound my thoughts worse than thy sword my 85
    flesh.
But thought's the slave of life, and life time's fool,
And time, that takes survey of all the world,
Must have a stop. O, I could prophesy,
But that the earthy and cold hand of death   90
Lies on my tongue. No, Percy, thou art dust,
And food for—   *[Dies.]*

102. **make so dear a show of zeal:** express admiration so ardently. **Dear** is often used to intensify meaning; see IV. i. 36 and other examples.

103. **favors:** personal insignia; e.g., colors.

112. **have a heavy miss of thee:** miss thee sadly.

119. **powder:** salt (to preserve the flesh).

121. **termagant:** savage. Termagant (or Tervagant) was believed to be the name of one of the gods of the Moslem races; **scot and lot:** lock, stock, and barrel; i.e., completely.

Prince. For worms, brave Percy. Fare thee well,
  great heart.
Ill-weaved ambition, how much art thou shrunk!   95
When that this body did contain a spirit,
A kingdom for it was too small a bound;
But now two paces of the vilest earth
Is room enough. This earth that bears thee dead
Bears not alive so stout a gentleman.   100
If thou wert sensible of courtesy,
I should not make so dear a show of zeal.
But let my favors hide thy mangled face;
And, even in thy behalf, I'll thank myself
For doing these fair rites of tenderness.   105
Adieu, and take thy praise with thee to heaven.
Thy ignominy sleep with thee in the grave,
But not rememb'red in thy epitaph.
                    He spieth Falstaff on the ground.
What, old acquaintance? Could not all this flesh
Keep in a little life? Poor Jack, farewell!   110
I could have better spared a better man.
O, I should have a heavy miss of thee
If I were much in love with vanity.
Death hath not struck so fat a deer today,
Though many dearer, in this bloody fray.   115
Emboweled will I see thee by and by;
Till then in blood by noble Percy lie.   *Exit.*
                              Falstaff riseth up.

Fal. Emboweled? If thou embowel me today, I'll
give you leave to powder me and eat me too tomorrow. 'Sblood, 'twas time to counterfeit, or that hot   120
termagant Scot had paid me scot and lot too. Coun-

127. **The better part of valor is discretion:** i.e., valor needs to be tempered by discretion. This idea was proverbial before Shakespeare, but is best known now in an inverse form of his phraseology, though it is usually understood to mean that discretion is preferable to valor.

129. **gunpowder:** violent.

133-34. **Nothing confutes me but eyes:** i.e., only a witness could confute my story.

138. **fleshed:** given a first taste of blood to; initiated.

144. **fantasy:** fancy.

147. **a double man:** a pun—I am neither two men nor the ghost of one. An apparition was sometimes called a **double man.**

terfeit? I lie; I am no counterfeit. To die is to be a
counterfeit, for he is but the counterfeit of a man
who hath not the life of a man; but to counterfeit
dying when a man thereby liveth is to be no counter-   125
feit but the true and perfect image of life indeed.
The better part of valor is discretion, in the which
better part I have saved my life. Zounds, I am afraid
of this gunpowder Percy, though he be dead. How
if he should counterfeit too, and rise? By my faith, I   130
am afraid he would prove the better counterfeit.
Therefore I'll make him sure; yea, and I'll swear I
killed him. Why may not he rise as well as I? Nothing confutes me but eyes, and nobody sees me. Therefore, sirrah [*Stabs him*], with a new wound in your   135
thigh, come you along with me.

                    He takes up Hotspur on his back.

[Re-]enter *Prince,* and *John of Lancaster.*

Prince. Come, brother John; full bravely hast thou
    fleshed
Thy maiden sword.
John.   But, soft! whom have we here?   140
Did you not tell me this fat man was dead?
Prince. I did; I saw him dead,
Breathless and bleeding on the ground. Art thou alive,
Or is it fantasy that plays upon our eyesight?
I prithee speak. We will not trust our eyes   145
Without our ears. Thou art not what thou seemst.
Fal. No, that's certain, I am not a double man; but

148. **Jack:** knave; see III. iii. 87.
166. **do thee grace:** bring thee favor.

113

if I be not Jack Falstaff, then am I a Jack. There is
Percy. If your father will do me any honor, so; if not,
let him kill the next Percy himself. I look to be either 150
earl or duke, I can assure you.

Prince. Why, Percy I killed myself, and saw thee
dead!

Fal. Didst thou? Lord, Lord, how this world is
given to lying. I grant you I was down, and out of 155
breath, and so was he; but we rose both at an instant
and fought a long hour by Shrewsbury clock. If I
may be believed, so; if not, let them that should reward valor bear the sin upon their own heads. I'll
take it upon my death, I gave him this wound in the 160
thigh. If the man were alive and would deny it,
zounds! I would make him eat a piece of my sword.

John. This is the strangest tale that ever I heard.

Prince. This is the strangest fellow, brother John.
Come, bring your luggage nobly on your back. 165
For my part, if a lie may do thee grace,
I'll gild it with the happiest terms I have.

　　　　　　　　　　　　A retreat is sounded.

The trumpet sounds retreat; the day is ours.
Come, brother, let's to the highest of the field,
To see what friends are living, who are dead. 170

　　　　　Exeunt [Prince Henry and Prince John].

Fal. I'll follow, as they say, for reward. He that re-
wards me, God reward him. If I do grow great, I'll
grow less; for I'll purge, and leave sack, and live
cleanly, as a nobleman should do.

　　　　　　　　　　Exit [bearing off the body].

V. [v.] Hotspur is dead and Worcester and Douglas are captured. Prince Hal, receiving from his father the right to deal with Douglas, awards the honor to his brother John and enjoins him to free Douglas without ransom.

The King then orders Prince John and Westmoreland to head for York to encounter Northumberland and Scroop, while he and Prince Hal go to Wales to cope with Glendower and Mortimer.

▄▄▄▄▄▄▄▄▄▄▄▄▄▄▄▄▄▄▄▄▄▄▄▄▄▄

5. **Misuse the tenor of thy kinsman's trust:** i.e., deceive thy kinsman (Hotspur).

12. **patiently:** stoically; with resignation.

15. **pause upon:** i.e., sit in later judgment on.

20. **Upon the foot of fear:** in cowardly flight.

Scene [V. Another part of the field.]

The trumpets sound. Enter the *King, Prince of Wales,
Lord John of Lancaster, Earl of Westmoreland,*
with *Worcester* and *Vernon* prisoners.

King. Thus ever did rebellion find rebuke.
Ill-spirited Worcester, did not we send grace,
Pardon, and terms of love to all of you?
And wouldst thou turn our offers contrary?
Misuse the tenor of thy kinsman's trust?   5
Three knights upon our party slain today,
A noble earl, and many a creature else
Had been alive this hour,
If like a Christian thou hadst truly borne
Betwixt our armies true intelligence.   10
Wor. What I have done my safety urged me to;
And I embrace this fortune patiently,
Since not to be avoided it falls on me.
King. Bear Worcester to the death, and Vernon too;
Other offenders we will pause upon.   15
        Exeunt Worcester and Vernon, [*guarded*].
How goes the field?
Prince. The noble Scot, Lord Douglas, when he saw
The fortune of the day quite turned from him,
The noble Percy slain, and all his men
Upon the foot of fear, fled with the rest;   20
And falling from a hill, he was so bruised
That the pursuers took him. At my tent

27. **honorable bounty:** act of kindness which will do you honor.

37. **bend you:** turn yourselves; **dearest:** greatest.

45. **leave:** leave off; stop.

The Douglas is, and I beseech your Grace
I may dispose of him.
    King.   With all my heart.   25
    Prince. Then, brother John of Lancaster, to you
This honorable bounty shall belong.
Go to the Douglas and deliver him
Up to his pleasure, ransomless and free.
His valors shown upon our crests today   30
Have taught us how to cherish such high deeds,
Even in the bosom of our adversaries.
    John. I thank your Grace for this high courtesy,
Which I shall give away immediately.
    King. Then this remains, that we divide our power. 35
You, son John, and my cousin Westmoreland,
Towards York shall bend you with your dearest speed
To meet Northumberland and the prelate Scroop,
Who, as we hear, are busily in arms.
Myself and you, son Harry, will towards Wales   40
To fight with Glendower and the Earl of March.
Rebellion in this land shall lose his sway,
Meeting the check of such another day;
And since this business so fair is done,
Let us not leave till all our own be won.   45
                                    Exeunt.

KEY TO

Famous Passages

So shaken as we are, so wan with care,
Find we a time for frighted peace to pant
And breathe short-winded accents of new broils
To be commenced in stronds afar remote.   [*King*—I. i. 1-4]

Before I knew thee, Hal, I knew nothing; and now am I . . .
   little better than one of the wicked.   [*Falstaff*—I. ii. 94-7]

Came there a certain lord, his chin new reaped
Showed like a stubble land at harvest home. . . .
                                      [*Hotspur*—I. iii. 34-71]

To put down Richard, that sweet lovely rose,
And plant this thorn, this canker, Bolingbroke.
                                      [*Hotspur*—I. iii. 184-85]

By heaven, methinks it were an easy leap
To pluck bright honor from the pale-faced moon. . . .
                                      [*Hotspur*—I. iii. 211-18]

Out of this nettle, danger, we pluck this flower,
   safety.   [*Hotspur*—II. iii. 9-10]

I am not yet of Percy's mind, the Hotspur of the North;
   he that kills me some six or seven dozen of Scots at a
   breakfast, washes his hands, and says to his wife,
   "Fie upon this quiet life! I want work."   [*Prince*—II. iv. 103-07]

Thou seest I have more flesh than another man, and
   therefore more frailty.   [*Falstaff*—III. iii. 169-71]

What is honor? A word. . . . Honor is a mere scutcheon—
   and so ends my catechism.   [*Falstaff*—V. i. 136-43]

Thought's the slave of life, and life time's fool,
And time, that takes survey of all the world,
Must have a stop.   [*Hotspur*—V. iv. 87-9]

The better part of valor is discretion.   [*Falstaff*—V. iv. 127]